HANS URS VON BALTHASAR

OUTSTANDING CHRISTIAN THINKERS

Series Editor: Brian Davies OP

The series offers a range of authoritative studies on people who have made an outstanding contribution to Christian thought and understanding. The series will range across the full spectrum of Christian thought to include Catholic and Protestant thinkers, to cover East and West, historical and contemporary figures. By and large, each volume will focus on a single 'thinker', but occasionally the subject may be a movement or a school of thought.

Brian Davies, OP, the Series Editor, is Regent of Studies at Blackfriars, Oxford, where he also teaches philosophy. He is a member of the Theology Faculty at the University of Oxford and tutor at St Benet's Hall, Oxford. He has lectured regularly at the University of Bristol, Fordham University, New York, and the Beda College, Rome. He is Reviews Editor of *New Blackfriars*. His previous publications include: *An Introduction to the Philosophy of Religion* (OUP, 1982); *Thinking about God* (Geoffrey Chapman, 1985); *The Thought of Thomas Aquinas* (OUP, 1992); and he was editor of *Language, Meaning and God* (Geoffrey Chapman, 1987).

Already published

The Apostolic Fathers
Simon Tugwell OP

Bultmann
David Fergusson

Denys the Areopagite
Andrew Louth

Reinhold Niebuhr
Kenneth Durkin

The Venerable Bede
Benedicta Ward SLG

Karl Rahner
William V. Dych SJ

Anselm
G. R. Evans

Lonergan
Frederick E. Crowe SJ

Teresa of Avila
Rowan Williams

Hans Urs von Balthasar
John O'Donnell SJ

Handel
Hamish Swanston

Yves Congar
Aidan Nichols OP

Planned titles in the series include:

Jonathan Edwards
John E. Smith

HANS URS VON BALTHASAR

John O'Donnell SJ

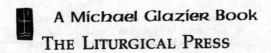
A Michael Glazier Book
THE LITURGICAL PRESS

Caro Amico Laurentio
in Domino

A Michael Glazier Book
published by The Liturgical Press
St John's Abbey, Collegeville, MN 56321, USA

Published in Great Britain by Geoffrey Chapman, an imprint of
Cassell Publishers Limited

First published 1992

Library of Congress Cataloging-in-Publication Data
A catalog record for this book is available from the Library of Congress.

ISBN 0-8146-5039-2

Typeset by Colset Private Limited, Singapore
Printed and bound in Great Britain by
Biddles Ltd, Guildford and King's Lynn

Contents

Editorial foreword

St Anselm of Canterbury once described himself as someone with faith seeking understanding. In words addressed to God he says 'I long to understand in some degree thy truth, which my heart believes and loves. For I do not seek to understand that I may believe, but I believe in order to understand.'

And this is what Christians have always inevitably said, either explicitly or implicitly. Christianity rests on faith, but it also has content. It teaches and proclaims a distinctive and challenging view of reality. It naturally encourages reflection. It is something to think about; something about which one might even have second thoughts.

But what have the greatest Christian thinkers said? And is it worth saying? Does it engage with modern problems? Does it provide us with a vision to live by? Does it make sense? Can it be preached? Is it believable?

This series originates with questions like these in mind. Written by experts, it aims to provide clear, authoritative and critical accounts of outstanding Christian writers from New Testament times to the present. It will range across the full spectrum of Christian thought to include Catholic and Protestant thinkers, thinkers from East and West, thinkers ancient, mediaeval and modern.

The series draws on the best scholarship currently available, so it will interest all with a professional concern for the history of Christian ideas. But contributors will also be writing for general readers who have little or no previous knowledge of the subjects to be dealt with. Volumes to appear should therefore prove helpful at a popular as well as an academic level. For the most part they will be devoted to a single thinker, but occasionally the subject will be a movement or school of thought.

Hans Urs von Balthasar, named as a Cardinal just before his death, was once a Jesuit. And, as John O'Donnell shows, he is important as a modern Ignatian theologian, along with Karl Rahner, whose work is documented by William Dych in a companion volume of the *Outstanding Christian Thinkers* series. But, as readers will also quickly discover, Balthasar's voluminous writings, like the writings of all the greatest Christian thinkers, deal with the whole Christian mystery seen as a complex totality. The significance of Scripture, the notion of creation, the nature and purpose of people, the meaning of faith, the nature and work of Christ: these are all topics on which Balthasar has written. And, as professional theologians generally recognize, his contribution to our understanding of them is both original and valuable. He stands as a major figure among twentieth-century Christian authors.

Balthasar is only now beginning to be studied by those who can only read him in English. Translations of his major works have been made only in the last twenty years or so, and there is no substantial English introduction to his thinking accessible to students and general readers. In what follows, Fr O'Donnell deals with the entire range of Balthasar's achievement in a clear and enthusiastic way. His book will therefore meet a serious need and is much to be welcomed as a means of approaching someone whose stature will doubtless continue to grow among Christians as time goes on.

Brian Davies OP

Bibliography

A complete bibliography of von Balthasar's works can be found in *Hans Urs von Balthasar: Bibliographie 1925–1990*, ed. Cornelia Capol (Einsiedeln: Johannes, 1990). The works listed below are those which have appeared thus far in English.

Christian Meditation (San Francisco: Ignatius Press, 1989).
The Christian State of Life (San Francisco: Ignatius Press, 1983).
Church and World (New York: Herder and Herder, 1967).
Convergences: To the Sources of the Christian Mystery (San Francisco: Ignatius Press, 1984).
Dare We Hope That All Men Be Saved? (San Francisco: Ignatius Press, 1988).
Does Jesus Know Us? Do We Know Him? (San Francisco: Ignatius Press, 1983).
Elizabeth of Dijon (London: Harvill Press, 1956).
Elucidations (London: SPCK, 1975).
Engagement with God (London: SPCK, 1975).
First Glance at Adrienne von Speyr (San Francisco: Ignatius Press, 1981).
The Glory of the Lord: A Theological Aesthetics, ed. Joseph Fessio and John Riches (Edinburgh: T. and T. Clark/San Francisco: Ignatius Press):
1: *Seeing the Form* (1985);
2: *Studies in Theological Styles: Clerical Styles* (1984);
3: *Studies in Theological Styles: Lay Styles* (1986);
4: *The Realm of Metaphysics in Antiquity* (1989);
5: *The Realm of Metaphysics in the Modern Age* (1990);
6: *Theology: The Old Covenant* (1990);
7: *Theology: The New Covenant* (1989).

The God Question and Modern Man (New York: Seabury, 1967).

The Heart of the World (San Francisco: Ignatius Press, 1980).

In the Fullness of Faith: On the Centrality of the Distinctively Catholic (San Francisco: Ignatius Press, 1988).

Life out of Death: Meditation on the Easter Mystery (Philadelphia: Fortress Press, 1985).

Love Alone. The Way of Revelation (London: Burns and Oates, 1968).

Man in History (London: Sheed and Ward, 1967).

Martin Buber and Christianity (London: Harvill Press, 1961).

Mary for Today (San Francisco: Ignatius Press, 1988).

The Moment of Christian Witness (New York: Newman Press, 1968).

Mysterium Paschale (Edinburgh: T. and T. Clark, 1990).

New Elucidations (San Francisco: Ignatius Press, 1986).

The Office of Peter and the Structure of the Church (San Francisco, Ignatius Press, 1989).

Prayer (San Francisco: Ignatius Press, 1987).

A Short Primer for Unsettled Laymen (San Francisco: Ignatius Press, 1985).

Test Everything, Hold Fast to What is Good (San Francisco: Ignatius Press, 1989).

Theodrama: Theological Dramatic Theory I: *Prolegomena* (San Francisco: Ignatius Press, 1988).

Theodrama: Theological Dramatic Theory II: *Dramatis Personae: Man in God* (San Francisco: Ignatius Press, 1990).

The Theology of Karl Barth (New York: Rinehart and Winston, 1971).

A Theology of History (London: Sheed and Ward, 1963).

Thérèse of Lisieux. A Story of a Mission (London: Sheed and Ward, 1953).

The Threefold Garland (San Francisco: Ignatius Press, 1982).

Truth is Symphonic: Aspects of Christian Pluralism (San Francisco: Ignatius Press, 1987).

You Crown the Year With Your Goodness: Sermons Through the Liturgical Year (San Francisco: Ignatius Press, 1989).

The Way of the Cross (London: Burns and Oates, 1969).

Who Is a Christian? (New York: Newman Press, 1968).

The Word Made Flesh (San Francisco: Ignatius Press, 1989).

Secondary literature

G. F. O'Hanlon, *The Immutability of God in the Theology of Hans Urs von Balthasar* (Cambridge University Press, 1990).

J. Riches (ed.), *The Analogy of Beauty: The Theology of Hans Urs von Balthasar* (Edinburgh: T. and T. Clark, 1986).

J. Saward, *The Mysteries of March: Hans Urs von Balthasar on the Incarnation and Easter* (London: Collins, 1990).

See also the issue of *Communio: International Catholic Review* (Fall 1989) devoted to articles on the theology of Balthasar.

1

Who is Hans Urs von Balthasar?

BIOGRAPHY[1]

Hans Urs von Balthasar was born into a well-established Catholic family of the city of Lucerne, Switzerland on 12 August 1905. Already as a boy he showed a remarkable interest in literature and talent for music, especially for the piano. After secondary schooling under the tutelage of the Benedictines and the Jesuits, he pursued doctoral studies in Zurich, Berlin and Vienna completing his dissertation on the theme of apocalyptic in German literature, before entering the novitiate of the Society of Jesus. During his Jesuit formation, Balthasar was to pursue theological studies at the Jesuit theologate at Lyons in France where he came under the influence of Henri de Lubac (1896-1991) with whom he began a lifelong friendship. For a time after his ordination to the priesthood he worked for the Jesuit magazine *Stimmen der Zeit* in Munich. Faced with the decision of whether he should pursue a career as a theological professor or devote himself to pastoral work and writing, he opted for the latter and was assigned as student chaplain to the University of Basel in 1940. It was there that he met Adrienne von Speyr, whom he accompanied in her journey to the Catholic Church.[2] After her reception into the Church, Balthasar became her spiritual director. Although he was the spiritual father, he was deeply impressed with what he judged to be her mystical experiences and he was convinced that she possessed a unique mission for the Church. With her he founded the secular institute,[3] the Community of St John (*Johannesgemeinschaft*).

1

Balthasar's role as director of the institute led to the most painful decision of his life, the decision to leave the Jesuit Order to whose spirituality he remained indebted and to which he remained linked by a bond of spiritual friendship. After his departure from the Jesuits he suffered a period of extreme isolation, was never offered a chair of theology and was not called to participate in the Second Vatican Council. In the years following the Council, his work gradually won recognition and in 1984 he received the Paul VI prize for theology. Intensely loyal to Rome and to the person of John Paul II, he was to have been created a Cardinal in June 1988, but two days before the consistory he died unexpectedly on the morning of 26 June 1988.

In this book we are concerned chiefly to present an introduction to Balthasar's theological vision. But if we look at the *ensemble* of his life, we must admit that Balthasar's contribution to the Church cannot be limited to theology. According to his own testimony, the driving force of his life was to contribute to the renewal of the Church. Especially in the early years he sought to do this by breaking down the walls which separated the Church from the world and by creating a dialogue between faith and culture. From this conviction arose his attachment to the idea of a secular institute which would have the mission to live the evangelical counsels in the midst of the world. In this way he hoped that the Community of St John could appropriate the Ignatian charism for the twentieth century. In later years his pastoral concern motivated him to involvement in the post-conciliar movements such as Comunione e Liberazione.[4]

Thus, in addition to his theological work, Balthasar expended his energies on numerous other activities for the renewal of the Church. Among these one could mention his work as a director of the *Spiritual Exercises* of St Ignatius of Loyola (1491–1556).[5] Then there was his task as a publisher. He opened his own publishing house to make available to the public works of spiritual and theological importance for the dialogue with culture. Balthasar not only served as editor of the press but also became a devoted translator. In this capacity he translated and edited important patristic texts such as those of the great Eastern Father of the Church, Origen (*c.* 185–*c.* 254) He also became one of the foremost translators of French Catholic literary figures such as Claudel (1868–1955), Péguy (1873–1914) and Bernanos (1888–1948). Convinced of the unique mission of Adrienne von Speyr, he devoted enormous energy to transcribing her works from personal dictations and undertook to publish the collected works, thus sacrificing time and energy which he could

2

have devoted to his own theological project. Before turning to a brief description of Balthasar's published corpus, let us look briefly at the major influences upon his theological creativity.

INFLUENCES

As I mentioned above, a decisive formative factor upon Balthasar's theology was his encounter at Lyons with Henri de Lubac. Here he came into contact with the so-called movement of the *nouvelle théologie* which sought to overcome the manual tradition of a dried and decadent scholasticism and to return to the rich patristic heritage of theology. The faculty of Lyons nurtured in Balthasar a love for the Fathers of the Church which prompted him to undertake several significant studies such as that devoted to Gregory of Nyssa (*c*. 330–*c*. 395) and Maximus the Confessor (*c*. 580–662). The *nouvelle théologie* also wanted to overcome the sharp division between nature and grace as well as the view which saw grace as something merely added onto a human nature already complete in itself. Such a view would seem to indicate that a human being could be perfectly fulfilled without God's offer of himself. According to the *nouvelle théologie* the human being is created with a dynamism toward the life of grace so that one finds one's humanity in accepting God's offer of grace.

Also important for this school was an accent upon the universal saving will of God. This vision which has firm roots in patristic theologians such as Origen has profound consequences for dialogue with culture and with the other religions, affects as well the Church's understanding of itself and its mission and has wide-ranging effects for the Christian community's way of living its faith. Universalism remained an abiding concern of Balthasar's to the end of his life, and in connection with Adrienne von Speyr's interpretation of the descent of Christ into hell, became one of the building blocks of Balthasar's theological edifice. One of Balthasar's last books, *Dare We Hope That All Men Be Saved?*,[6] returned to this leitmotiv of his theology.

A second decisive influence upon Balthasar was the Jesuit philosopher Erich Przywara (1889–1972). Balthasar came to know Przywara during his tenure in Munich in the years after his priestly ordination and once said that he was the greatest mind he was ever privileged to meet. Przywara shaped Balthasar's philosophical inquiry. While colleagues of Balthasar's such as Karl Rahner

3

(1904–84) were turning to German idealism for philosophical inspiration, under Przywara's influence, Balthasar moved in another direction. The key philosophical idea of Przywara which made an impression upon Balthasar was that of the analogy of being which Przywara regarded as the key principle of interpretation in Catholic thinking.

According to the doctrine of analogy there is a relationship of similarity between the creature and God insofar as all creatures proceed from God and must therefore in some way resemble him. Although Catholic philosophy and theology had perennially made use of the doctrine of analogy, Pryzwara gave it new life by interpreting the analogy of being in a dynamic rather than in a static way. Every creature is a dynamism toward God. As a creature it resembles the creator but in its dynamism toward the creator, the creature experiences an ever-greater *excessus* toward the Transcendent who recedes with every approach of the creature. Far from capturing God in human categories, the doctrine of analogy preserves the transcendence of God and reveals God to be the ever-greater one. Przywara thus places the doctrine of analogy within the framework of negative theology. His philosophy has the merit of reviving for Catholic theology the principle of analogy enunciated by the Fourth Lateran Council (1215), 'For all the similarity between God and the creature, there exists an ever-greater dissimilarity'. This principle, so important for Balthasar, became a cardinal point in his discussions with the great Protestant champion of neo-orthodoxy, Karl Barth (1886–1968).

For Karl Barth, the doctrine of the analogy of being represented the anti-Christ and the most serious obstacle to becoming a Catholic. Barth's motive for taking this strong polemical position was that he believed that the doctrine of analogy introduced two sources into theology, a philosophical source of knowledge about God and one that derived from faith. For Barth, all knowledge of God is derived from Christ. As the category of covenant began to play an increasing role in his theology, Barth modified his views on the role of creation in theology. Since the creation was willed by God from eternity and ordered to Christ, the world must also reflect God's glory. Nonetheless, Barth never retracted his views on the analogy of being and retained to the end his notion that the only valid principle of analogy in theology is the analogy of faith.

Balthasar was attracted to Barth's Christocentrism and sought to interpret his theology in a favourable light. Balthasar went so far as to seek to integrate the analogy of being into the analogy of faith.

Nonetheless, he retained the view that the analogy of being was a necessary presupposition for the analogy of faith, since only through the analogy of being could one preserve the liberty of the creature without which a genuine covenant would be impossible. According to Balthasar, Barth's analogy of faith without an analogy of being was in danger of becoming a monologue between God and himself.

One of Barth's great contributions to Protestant theology was to overcome Calvin's doctrine of double predestination. According to Calvin (1509–64) some persons are predestined by God from eternity to eternal happiness and others to eternal damnation. For Barth, on the other hand, there is only one election of the human race, its election in Christ. Although Barth's theology was in many ways a trenchant critique of liberal theology which sought to reconcile the Christian gospel with the values of modern culture, the universalism implied in his doctrine of election made dialogue with the world possible. We have already seen that Balthasar was inspired by the Fathers' teaching on the universal saving will of God, and Barth's teaching confirmed Balthasar's instincts in this direction. Another feature of Barth's theology which made a *rapprochement* with Balthasar's thinking possible was his emphasis upon the humiliation of the Son in the incarnation and the paschal mystery. Barth's theology, centred on the cross of Christ and emphasizing the obedience of the Son, accorded perfectly with the insights which Balthasar was learning from Adrienne von Speyr.

Without a doubt the most decisive influence upon Balthasar after 1940 was Adrienne von Speyr. As Balthasar attests, it is impossible to separate her thinking from his, so great did the two modes of theologizing merge into a synthesis. One way of seeing their relation is to attribute the creative insights to Adrienne, and to Balthasar the filtering of these insights through the theological tradition of the Church. Among the theological impulses which he inherited from her, we could mention the following: Christ's descent into hell as his solidarity with the abandoned, Jesus's Sonship as obedience to the point of powerless identification with the Godforsaken, faith as Marian womb-like receptivity, virginity as spiritual fruitfulness for the world, personhood as unique sending from God, the vicarious representative character of prayer and suffering in the Church, the bodiliness of Christian existence, the naked standing before God and the Church in the sacramental act of confession as expressing the fundamental Christian attitude. To many of these themes we will return in the course of this book, since they offer Balthasar important interpretive principles for understanding Christian doctrines.

Finally, we should mention the historically distant but theologically and spiritually proximate influence of Ignatius of Loyola. Balthasar's entire theological project was developed under the guiding inspiration of the *Spiritual Exercises* of St Ignatius. In addition to Ignatius's stress upon interior liberty, indifference and obedience, as well as his Christocentric mysticism and incarnational spirituality, it was probably the Ignatian desire to find God in all things which inspired Balthasar the most. One could sum up Ignatius's spirituality in the maxim 'With God in the world'. Just as the secular institute, the Community of St John, was meant to live out this truth, so Balthasar's thought was meant to elaborate the theological underpinnings for the spirituality embodied in this maxim, the spirituality which Balthasar believed was required for living Christian faith in today's secular world.

BEING AS LOVE[7]

Before indicating the structure of Balthasar's theological project, it could be helpful to indicate the question which guides his research and the principal intuition which underlies his theological synthesis. Martin Heidegger (1889–1976) has urged that the most pressing philosophical question is the Being-question. Heidegger's thought pivots around what he calls the ontological difference, the difference between Being and beings. Beings are the entities that are. Being is what lets beings be. Heidegger once compared Being to the lighting up of a clear space in the midst of a forest. The uniqueness of human being (*Dasein*) is that humans can question their Being. They are the being for whom Being itself is an issue. This lighting up of Being for human beings distinguishes them from things like tables and chairs.

One could also say that for Balthasar the Being-question is the dominating leitmotiv of his thought. The Western philosophical tradition, especially as it flowered in German idealism, has responded to the Being-question by affirming that Being is Spirit. By Spirit is meant self-consciousness, being-present-to-oneself. According to this tradition the ultimate reality is God who is conceived as Absolute Spirit or Absolute Self-Presence. Balthasar's fundamental intuition is that Christianity leads us in another direction. The Christian revelation leads us to the affirmation that Being is love. Being is the trinitarian love of the Father and the Son in the Holy Spirit. Hence the prime analogue in human experience for the illumination of Being will not be the subject's presence to self but the presence of the Thou to the I.

For Balthasar, as for all the great philosophers as well as theologians, the fundamental question is the value of the world in which we live and the meaning of our temporal existence. The fundamental intuition which guides his thinking is that it is possible to live in this world without being broken by its tensions because the origin from which the world flows and the goal toward which it is moving is the triune God understood as the infinite community of love. Being is ecstatic love, the love of the Trinity open to the world. Because the world has its place in God, everything in it is destined to be preserved. The great insight of Christian faith, which opens up a vista beyond the ultimately world-denying way of Eastern religions and the pessimistic way of modern atheism, is that wordly *eros* is to be redeemed by *caritas*. Here Dante (1265–1321) becomes a figure of supreme importance with his vision that Beatrice precedes him into paradise. In Christ we see that our worldly loves are not to be left behind but are to be integrated into heavenly ones. Time will find its fulfilment in eternity.

It is sometimes said that Balthasar's theology is so elitist and faith-centred that it has nothing to say to those outside the Church. But such an objection misses, I believe, the fundamental thrust of Balthasar's theological project. At root, Balthasar's approach is meant to open a dialogue with the great Western philosophical tradition as well as with the great mystical tradition of the East. Although Balthasar believes that Christian faith ultimately offers an alternative to these traditions, such an alternative does not entail a radical rejection of them. Their elements of truth must be preserved and integrated into the Christian vision. Christ, as the absolute saviour, not only judges all other redeemers but integrates them into himself.

THE THEOLOGICAL PROJECT

Since the Being-question is Balthasar's driving inspiration, the reality of Being offers the scaffolding upon which Balthasar seeks to create a new theological synthesis. Here the cardinal affirmation is that Being is the transcendental reality as such. The classical philosophical tradition affirmed four attributes as the transcendental

7

properties of Being: unity, goodness, truth and beauty. These transcendental properties provide the structure for Balthasar's theological project. In his earliest *chef d'oeuvre*, *The Glory of the Lord*, Balthasar unfolds in seven volumes the theological nature of divine beauty. He explores how divine glory is reflected in the face of Christ especially in his cross and resurrection, and how the Christian tradition has sought to give creative expression to this aesthetic dimension of faith. In the *Theodramatik* in five volumes the accent shifts to the good. Here in the centre of the discussion stands the problem of liberty, God's freedom and ours. The encounter of these two freedoms constitutes the drama of salvation history. Finally, in the last part of the trilogy, the *Theologik* in three volumes, Balthasar turns his attention to the problem of the truth of Being. Here he focuses upon three questions. First, what is the philosophical nature of truth? Second, how is it possible to make the leap from a philosophical account of truth to Jesus' astounding claim to be the truth in person? Finally, how does the Holy Spirit lead us into the truth of Christ?

Such is the goal of Balthasar's theological programme which indicates the path we must follow in order to arrive at a basic comprehension of his theological vision. Having situated Balthasar's theological endeavour within the context of twentieth-century theology and having espied his fundamental intuition, let us commence our journey together by turning our attention to Balthasar's tireless effort to determine the nature of the Catholic and his lifelong concern to show how Jesus Christ in his person and mission incarnates the meaning of catholicity.

Notes

1   For Balthasar's own account of his life and work, see 'In retrospect' and 'Another ten years—1975' in *The Analogy of Beauty*, ed. John Riches (Edinburgh: T. and T. Clark, 1986), pp. 194–221, 222–33. A very useful introduction to the influences upon Balthasar's thought can be found in *The von Balthasar Reader*, ed. Medard Kehl and Werner Löser (Edinburgh: T. and T. Clark, 1982), pp. 3–54. See also Hans Urs von Balthasar, *Unser Auftrag* (Einsiedeln: Johannes, 1984).

2   Adrienne von Speyr (1902–67) was a medical doctor. She was brought up in a Protestant household, and was twice married. Grieving for the death of her first husband, she found it impossible to pray the Lord's prayer; Balthasar helped her to see that praying 'thy will be done' is not a human achievement but an opening of ourselves to what God wishes to do in us. In addition to the gift of clairvoyance and the charism of healing, she received extraordinary graces in prayer. Dictating to

Balthasar every day, she commented on the great works of sacred scripture. These dictations, later edited and published by Balthasar, are the result not of theological study (she never had any formal theological education) but of her personal insights in prayer.

3   A secular institute is a community in which the members take vows of poverty, chastity and obedience but live in the world and follow a secular profession. Their consecration remains hidden. For Balthasar, the way of life of the secular institute represents the Johannine theology of the seed falling into the ground and dying in order to bear much fruit. In spite of the seed's hiddenness, union with Christ guarantees a fecundity which perhaps will only be revealed in the world to come.

4   Comunione e Liberazione is a movement of lay people, especially strong in Europe, which stresses the active and public commitment of Christians in all forms of secular activity such as politics and the arts.

5   The *Spiritual Exercises* offer a structured period of prayer of about thirty days' duration during which the retreatant is led progressively to a deeper commitment to Christ and often to a choice of a state of life. Ideally the retreatant is accompanied by a director with whom he meets each day to discuss the progress of his prayer.

6   *Dare We Hope That All Men Be Saved?* (San Francisco: Ignatius Press, 1988).

7   I would argue that the central insight of Balthasar's entire thought can be summed up in the proposition that Being is love. See, for example, 'Der Zugang zur Wirklichkeit Gottes' in *Mysterium Salutis* 2: *Die Heilsgeschichte vor Christus*, ed. Johannes Feiner and Magnus Löhrer (Benziger, 1967), pp. 15–43. See also Werner Löser, 'Unangefochtene Kirchlichkeit—universaler Horizont', *Herder Korrespondenz* (October 1988), p. 477.

2

The search for catholicity[1]

INTRODUCTION

As we saw in the first chapter, the question which has guided
Balthasar's theological reflection is the same question which has
motivated philosophers over the centuries, namely the question of
Being. What does it mean to be? For Balthasar, this problem is intimately related to the classical problem of the One and the Many,
which goes back as far as the pre-Socratic philosophers and Plato.
In his opinion the solution can ultimately be found only in Christ.
He is the point where the one and the many, the universal and the
concrete, form a perfect synthesis. Balthasar's way of proceeding in
this reflection is confrontational. He considers the possible solutions to the radical human question of Being, playing off one solution against the other, until he can show that only Christ offers us
the true answer.

THE WAY OF THE RELIGIONS

Let us consider in turn three possible human responses to the problem of the One and the Many, all of which in Balthasar's opinion are
doomed to failure. First, let us consider the way of the religions. For
the religions, that is, the path of the pagans, the absolute consists in
the sphere of the gods. The pagan religions are essentially poly-
theistic. Balthasar would basically agree with Feuerbach (1804–72)
that the gods are projections of some aspect of human need onto the

sphere of the divine. For example, the gods offer protection from the perils of nature or defence in battle. In this vision the gods exist really for the service of human needs. People need the gods to deliver them from the powers which threaten them. Hence, as Balthasar says, the pagan religions have an inbuilt tendency toward magic. Human beings have a propulsion to manipulate the gods to serve their purposes.

Another feature of the pagan religions to which Balthasar frequently returns is mythology. Myths are significant because they attempt to relate the transcendent realm to space and time. Myths use the language of the world to speak about that which transcends the world. Hegel (1770–1831) thought of myths as a step to be transcended, as the human mind moved to the absolute truth of philosophy. But, in Balthasar's opinion, Schelling (1775–1854) is closer to the truth in maintaining that myth and philosophy form two parallel and indispensable approaches to the truth. Myths cannot be dispensed with since they represent the immanence of the divine in the cosmos. For Schelling, myth expresses the general in the particular. Christianity both does justice to the truth which myth seeks to express while at the same time transcending its inadequacy. On the one hand, Christianity affirms with myth that God is known in the world. Any approach to the divine which seeks to bypass the world is condemned to failure, for such an approach would neglect the concrete realm where men and women live. On the other hand, Christ transcends myth, for he is not the general in the particular. As we shall see, Christ is the *totality* (*das Ganze*) in the concrete. For Balthasar, Christ is not a particular. He is the unique (*einmalig*). We will develop this point in greater detail later in this chapter.

If, as we saw above, the religions have a tendency to degenerate into magic, it is equally true that the religions have an intrinsic propulsion to purification. Indeed, this is what we see in the history of religions. Gradually human intelligence sees that no aspect of the cosmos can be divinized. God must transcend the cosmos if he is truly God. Hence polytheism gives way to the religion of the One. Here we find the other side of the polarity, the search for a synthesis between the One and the Many which places the accent upon the One.

THE WAY OF NEGATION

In the history of human culture there are two great ways which propose a pilgrimage to the One. The first is that of the Eastern religions such as Buddhism. For Buddhism the world of ordinary experience, the world of finite beings, is really an illusion (*maya*). These things are nothing. In this world of illusion one is caught in the vicious circle of suffering. The way out is to recognize the illusory character of being, and by purification and meditation arrive at the really real, namely nothing. Buddhism does not offer a speculative solution to the problem of the One and the Many, rather it proposes a way, which is a way toward salvation. Still Buddhism is, in Balthasar's opinion, ultimately unsatisfactory, for it does not have an answer to how *maya* comes to be nor to why human existence consists of the tragic circle of suffering. Moreover, Buddhism proposes a solution which denies its own starting point, namely suffering men and women in the world. The solution to the world's suffering consists in denying the world.

The other great way to salvation, one which has significantly influenced Christianity, is that of Neo-Platonism. This is also a *via negativa*. The human being reaches the One by a long and arduous ascent; in this pilgrimage one must progressively deny that every creature is God and so by a way of negation one gradually surrenders to the ultimate source of unity which is beyond all creatures. Balthasar throughout his life was fascinated by this way which has such strong links with Christian mysticism. In this vision the world becomes a springboard which propels people to the divine. One leaves behind the mesmerizing light of creatures to arrive at the dazzling darkness of God.

But for all his fascination with this vision, and in spite of its element of truth, Balthasar recognizes that it is a defective solution. For the *via negativa* leaves us as well with a number of unanswered questions. Among the most pressing are the following: in the *via negativa* I can explain the movement from the many to the one but how do I explain the movement from the one to the many? Why does the one splinter itself into the many? Is this an overflow? Is it a fall? Is this splintering necessary? Secondly, is it possible to love an impersonal One? How can I love absolute nothingness? Finally, as in Buddhism, does this vision demand that I deny my own starting point in order to solve the enigma of myself? Am I to be fulfilled by dissolving myself in the impersonal absolute? Does the negation here outweigh the primordial affirmation of myself which I first received from my mother's smile?

HEGELIANISM

Having looked at a solution which is oriented to the many and at another solution which is oriented to the one, we can lastly consider a third option which presents itself in the history of culture, namely that of Hegel. It seems to me that Balthasar is less attracted to Hegel than he is to Neo-Platonism, but standing intellectually in the German philosophical tradition, he seems to feel bound to return often to the proposed Hegelian solution in order to show how the Christian answer surpasses it. Hegel too, like the great metaphysicians before him, seeks a way of synthesis between the one and the many. As is well known, his solution consists in the reality of Spirit, that is, thought thinking itself; thought becoming conscious of itself through finite realities. Hence the ultimate unity is Spirit but Spirit realizes its unity through a process of self-differentiation. Spirit produces an other, the world, as the means to become conscious of itself. Hence Hegel believes that his philosophy does justice to both the one and the many. The world of plurality, of finite beings, of suffering existence, is real but it exists as a moment of Absolute Spirit. The world is a necessary moment in God's self-expression.

As impressive as this solution is, Balthasar maintains that it is a spurious solution which does justice neither to God nor to man. First, he argues that Hegel's Absolute Spirit is not really God, for this God is not really transcendent since God needs the world in order to be God.

Secondly, for various reasons Hegel's philosophy does not do justice to human beings. In the first place, in the end the human being's concrete individuality is abolished, as the individual is subjected to become a moment of the Absolute. Secondly, Balthasar argues that Hegel does not do justice to the phenomenon of love. According to Balthasar, Hegel's reflections on love and friendship are profound but ultimately miss the mark. In Hegel's philosophy, the only way in which the subject can overcome its abstract self and become a concrete individual is by surrendering itself to another. Unless I place myself in relation to another, I can never achieve identity. Here Hegel comes very close to the Christian vision of people. I can only win myself by losing myself. The problem is whether in Hegel's vision the other is ever loved for his or her own sake, or is the other always a means for achieving my self-realization?

The whole problematic in Hegel is that of the isolated subject. The movement in his thought is from the One to the Other and back to the One. But is this not a subtle form of egoism? Is there not a subtle form of resentment in Hegel's philosophy? The subject has to die in order to realize itself. Friendship bears an element of resentment, because it calls for renunciation, a renunciation which the self must grudgingly make in order to win concrete identity. Thus, Balthasar would say that Hegel has not understood the phenomenon of love in its depths. He has made of it a logical necessity.

Finally, we could mention that Balthasar argues that Hegel does not offer an adequate approach to the reality of human suffering and death. Hegel tries to do justice to the negativity of suffering and death. But here once again he makes this negativity a moment in the Absolute's self-realization. This would seem to rob death of its seriousness, of its deadly destructive character. Is it not blasphemous to make the horrible reality of suffering and death a speculative necessity? Must not any philosophical account pale in the face of the sheer disproportion of such human suffering as that of the genocide of the death camps of Auschwitz and Birkenau? Can the so-called waste products of evolution and the millions of victims of war and persecution be explained as a necessary moment of absolute self-consciousness? Balthasar would argue that no speculative solution can give us the key to unravel the enigma of human existence and its suffering.

COMPETING CLAIMS TO CATHOLICITY

Thus far we have looked at three approaches to the problem of Being: the polytheism of the religions, the monism of Neo-Platonism and Buddhism, the dialectical philosophy of Hegel. All have proved wanting. Let us now see how in Christ the meaning of Being is unveiled. The nucleus of Balthasar's solution is simple. Jesus is the Catholic as such. By Catholic Balthasar means that Jesus is the most singular of human realities but a singular in whom the universal meaning of Being is revealed.

Before we can unfold this solution further, we must first of all note that Balthasar admits that here we confront the scandal of particularity. But Balthasar does not shy away from this scandal. In fact he maintains that we can only fully appreciate the catholicity of Christ if we place his claim to catholicity in confrontation with other such claims. In this sense Balthasar advocates a different type of ecumenism, not the eirenic ecumenism of watering down the truth but the serious confrontation of competing claims to truth.

His method is that of dialogue through confrontation and in arguing for this method he appeals to a saying of George Tyrrell (1861–1909), 'The law of competition prevails and stimulates development'. In the case of Christ, it is a question of a rivalry between different claims to embrace the totality of truth.

Balthasar situates Christ between two different claims to truth, the one vertical and the other horizontal. We already looked at the vertical claim to truth above in the path of the *via negativa*. This approach is vertical in that it attempts to leave the world behind in a direct flight to the One. The salvation offered by the vertical approach is world-denying.

For Balthasar, the second competitive claim for the totality of truth is found in Judaism. This is the horizontal approach. Judaism is firmly rooted in the reality of history and is an openness of history to the future. From Balthasar's point of view Judaism is already infinitely superior to the vertical way of salvation, for Israel's faith no longer represents the human struggle for salvation from below. Hebrew faith begins with the fact, as Abraham Heschel (1907–72) put it, that God is in search of humanity.

As I already noted, for Balthasar, the centre of Israel's faith is its openness to the future. Judaic faith is a faith centred on promise. But precisely here we encounter the difficulty in its claim to catholicity. On the one hand, as the religion of the future, Israel bears the promise of the future of all humanity. There is a strong universalistic tendency in Israelite faith. Israel is called to be the light to the nations. On the other hand, Israel remains bound to her racial origins. She remains a particular people. Here is the tension. If she opens herself outward as bearer of the promise for all, there is the danger of losing her identity. But in closing in upon herself, there is an equally grave danger of loss of identity by failing to bear the promise.

If we look at the concrete history of the Jewish people, we see that both of these dangers are verified. In the Zionist movement, for example, there is an idolatrous clinging to national identity. In Marxism, on the other hand, the messianic promise is so secularized that the original meaning of the promise is lost. Thus Balthasar believes that apart from faith in Christ Israel will always remain an enigma to herself. The tension between particularity and universality can only be overcome by the free unexpected gift of God's future in Christ.

Finally, we can note that for Balthasar both of these competing claims to catholicity have ended historically in atheism. The solution offered by Nirvana in Buddhism is essentially god-less. Even the Platonic One seems to be ultimately impersonal and incapable of a free relation with the world. The Marxist vision of the utopian future of the world is equally atheistic. Thus the coming of Christ provokes a decision. Concretely the man or woman of today stands between a choice of competing claims to catholicity and these claims can be reduced to two: either the atheism of the vertical and the horizontal way or the God of Jesus Christ.

But Balthasar also helps us to see that a choice of either of these forms of atheism involves a denial of the world. The vertical way denies the world by a flight from the world into Nothing. The horizontal way involves a denial of the world by placing salvation always ahead of man in the empty space of the future. The way of Jesus, on the other hand, is the way where the horizontal and the vertical meet. His is the way of the cross where God takes the world so seriously that he enters into the tragic contradictions of human existence.

JESUS CHRIST AS THE CATHOLIC

We are now in a position to clarify how Balthasar understands the assertion that Jesus is the Catholic as such. The essence of Balthasar's position is simple, namely, Jesus is the point where time and eternity meet. This is possible because Jesus is at one and the same time the eternal Logos (Word), and as Barth would put it, the eternally elected man; and he is equally the Logos in the flesh, fully inserted into human history. From the perspective of time, Christ our passover has been sacrificed (1 Cor 5:7); from the perspective of eternity, Jesus is the Lamb slaughtered before the foundation of the world (Rev 13:8). As temporal he bears the temporality of human existence; as eternal Logos he can make a claim to absolute meaning.

All of this is possible of course only within a trinitarian perspective. God is not the bare monad of Neo-Platonic philosophy. Rather God is the Father who eternally generates the Son in love and the Son is the eternal response of love to the Father. Hence the problem of the One and the Many goes back to the Trinity. The Christian God is a monotheistic God but not a monadic God. God from all eternity exists with his Other who is the Son. Otherness cannot be excluded from the ultimate reality. Since the Father is always with the Son, otherness has a positive value which can never be done

16

away with. Moreover, the otherness, which is the Son, makes possible the otherness of the world. On the one hand, the Son becomes the archetype of God's work of creation. On the other hand, the infinite space of love between the Father and the Son, which is the Holy Spirit, becomes the 'space' where the world is inserted.

God does not need the world to realize himself as in Hegelian philosophy since the Father is perfectly fulfilled in his self-gift to the Son. But it is equally true that neither the Father nor the Son keep their love for themselves. Their love bound together in the Holy Spirit is ecstatic—it is a love open to the world, to time, to history. And so Balthasar has shown, first, that Jesus is the Catholic *par excellence*, and secondly, that his catholicity is rooted in the Trinity. The triune unity of Father, Son and Holy Spirit is the mystery of the One and the Many which renders possible both the existence of the world and the incarnation of the Son in that world. Balthasar, as we saw at the beginning of this chapter, has consistently raised the philosophical question of the One and the Many, of essence and existence. In the end, his reflection leads to the affirmation that the Mystery of Being can only be unveiled from above in the gift of Christ and in his incarnation. In the light of this revelation it is also seen that the meaning of Being is trinitarian love.

Note

1 One of the principal sources for Balthasar's ideas on catholicity is his essay 'Anspruch auf Katholizität' in *Pneuma und Institution* (Einsiedeln: Johannes, 1974), pp. 61–116.

3

Faith as an aesthetic act

INTRODUCTION

One of the central concerns of Balthasar's theology is to recover the conviction that God is the supreme Beauty. The mystery of Christian faith consists in the fact that God who is Beauty as such and who dwells in inaccessible light has become visible to us in his Son Jesus Christ. Balthasar is fond of citing in this context the preface for the feast of Christmas, 'Through the mystery of the incarnate Word the new light of your brightness has shone onto the eyes of our mind, that knowing God visibly, we might be snatched up by this into the love of invisible things'.[1] If by virtue of the incarnation God has become visible, then it belongs to the nature of Christian faith to contemplate God's glory in the flesh. It is above all St John, Balthasar's favourite scriptural author, who accentuates this dimension of faith. An important text for Balthasar in this regard is 1 John 1:1–4:

> That which was from the beginning, which we have heard, which we have seen with our eyes, which we have looked upon and touched with our hands, concerning the word of life—the life was made manifest, and we saw it, and testify to it, and proclaim to you the eternal life which was with the Father and was made manifest to us—that which we have seen and heard we proclaim also to you, so that you may have fellowship with us; and our fellowship is with the Father and with his Son Jesus Christ.

18

If the centre of Christian faith is Jesus Christ as the appearance of the invisible God, then, according to Balthasar, Christian faith has of necessity a contemplative function. Believing consists in looking upon Jesus and seeing in him the glory of the Father. The believer must return ever anew to this wellspring of contemplation. He must continue to focus his gaze upon the incarnate and crucified Christ, there to be drawn into the mystery of the eternal Godhead. From this truth it follows that Christian theology must have a contemplative dimension. Christian theology is a reflection upon what has been seen with the eyes of faith. According to Balthasar, this conviction underpinned all the theological reflection of the patristic and mediaeval period. Such a conception of theology, however, was shattered with the discordant notes which entered theology with Luther (1483–1546) and the reformation and the breakdown of the mediaeval synthesis that followed Descartes (1596–1650) and flowered in modern philosophy. At the heart of Balthasar's entire theological programme is the desire to recover this aesthetic dimension for Christian dogmatics.

THE ELIMINATION OF THE AESTHETIC DIMENSION

The loss of the aesthetic dimension of theology can be traced to Luther. With the rise of the Reformation a sharp dichotomy was introduced into faith between hearing and seeing. For the Reformers, the heart of faith was listening to God's Word, not contemplating his appearance. For Luther, the mediaeval contemplative dimension was the result of a false introduction of Neo-Platonic philosophy into Christianity. Luther rejected in principle any idea of aesthetic harmony in theology. For him, Christian faith rested upon contradiction rather than upon harmony. The fact that God who is exalted becomes lowly, that the holy God identifies with the sinner, that the ever-living Lord dies on the cross—all these are contradictions that are stumbling blocks for reason and can only be accepted in faith. For Luther, at the heart of theology lies contradiction, or, as he so often expressed it, *Deus sub contrario*. As Balthasar notes, for Luther

No harmonizing, no skill is permitted. Every form which man tries to impose on revelation in order to achieve an overview that makes comprehension possible—for this is presupposed in beauty—every form must disintegrate in the face of the

19

'contradiction', the concealment of everything divine under its opposite, the concealment, that is, of all proportions and analogies between God and man in dialectic.[2]

Luther's rejection of the aesthetic has prevailed in Protestant theology even until our own day. Among its modern chief representatives is Kierkegaard (1813–55), for whom the aesthetic point of view and that of faith are opposed in the sharpest possible way. For Kierkegaard, the aesthetic is the epitome of that which is frivolous, capricious, lacking in seriousness. To this must be opposed the attitude of faith which is realized in radical interiority, the naked confrontation of the individual with God. Clearly in this perspective the dimension of the worldly and the communitarian is lost for faith. Only with Karl Barth is there a hint at the recovery of beauty for theology. Barth admitted that God is beautiful in a manner proper to him alone and indeed Barth had the courage to affirm God as the primal Beauty.

Nevertheless, Barth was unable fully to exploit this insight for three reasons. First, because he rejected the doctrine of the analogy of being and thus could not perceive any harmony between worldly beauty and divine beauty. Secondly, Barth's view of faith was actualistic, which is to say that faith exists only in the moment when one responds to the Word of God. Faith is thus a series of discrete acts. There is nothing which perdures as the source and object of contemplation. Finally, for Barth, the aesthetic dimension of faith is reserved for the *eschaton*. At the present, humankind lives in a world disfigured by sin which renders the divine beauty inaccessible.

If Protestant theology excluded the beautiful from faith, it is equally true that Catholic theology in the period after the collapse of the medieval synthesis failed to do justice to the aesthetic dimension of faith. Under the influence of Romanticism and German idealism, Catholic authors such as François René de Chateaubriand (1768–1848) and Alois Gügler (1782–1827) offered an apologetics based on aesthetic categories. Appealing to the Bible as poetry, the aesthetic dimension of the liturgy and the inner harmony of the Christian mysteries, they tried to justify Catholic Christianity, but according to Balthasar, they made the fatal error of taking inner-worldly standards of beauty as the criterion for the beauty of divine revelation. By contrast, Balthasar argues that the only legitimate way of proceeding to create a theological aesthetics is to let divine revelation set its own standards of beauty. Only by pursuing this hermeneutical principle can we avoid the trap of falling into an aesthetical theology.[3] For a theological aesthetics there is, to be sure, an analogy between worldly beauty and divine beauty. But the criterion for beauty remains always with God and his revelation. Balthasar remains a vigorous defender of the analogy of being[4] but he remains faithful to Barth to the extent that the analogy of being remains firmly situated within the analogy of faith.[5] The true measure of worldly beauty can be perceived only from the self-revelation of divine beauty.

ELEMENTS OF A THEOLOGICAL AESTHETICS

In an article on Balthasar's theological aesthetics, Louis Dupré observes that the basic hermeneutical principle guiding the Swiss theologian's analysis of glory is that the theological object provides the conditions of possibility for its knowledge. In other words, the conditions for the possibility of theological knowledge are the conditions that constitute the theological object itself.[6]

First, the theological object is constituted by the form of revelation by which the infinite and invisible God takes on contours in space and time. Moreover, the form is a *Gestalt*, that is, a totality which transcends the variety and diversity of its parts. The form of Christian revelation is nothing less than Jesus Christ. From this form emerges the second condition of possibility for theological knowledge, namely the light which draws the beholder into itself. The light is the ground of the experience of rapture, the experience by which the observer is seized by beauty and drawn into its dazzling radiance. Balthasar notes 'The beautiful is above all a *form*, and the light does not fall on this form from above and from outside, rather it breaks forth from the form's interior'.[7]

Later, Balthasar applies this category to the experience of faith when he writes 'The light of faith stems from the object which, revealing itself to the subject, draws it out beyond itself . . . into the sphere of the object'.[8] Thus, in the aesthetic experience of faith, the light emerging from the object, which is nothing less than the grace of God, enables the believer to see the form of revelation. The beholder is given the eyes of perception. In this sense, Dupré notes that Balthasar stands in the mystical tradition of Eckhart (*c.* 1260–1327) who taught that the eye which sees God is the eye with which God sees himself. In this perspective Balthasar observes that every experience of the beautiful involves a di-polarity. On the one hand, perceiving the form is the experience of a fullness. One is grasped by the harmony of the proportions. This aspect comes to the fore in classicism such as Greek art with its emphasis on geometrical shape in architecture and on ideal human form in sculpture. On the other hand, the perfection of form initiates the perceiver into an experience of depth which is reflected in the inexhaustible character of a work of art. A genuine work of art will never cease to attract, for it contains infinite depth. According to Balthasar, these aesthetic dimensions are realized to perfection in Jesus as the revelation of divine beauty. He is the perfection of divine form, in that the fullness of divine being exists in him bodily (Col 1:19). At the same time he draws us into the infinite depths of the Father who is the unfathomable origin of his being and the inexhaustible abyss from which everything has its being. With these principles in mind, let us turn to Balthasar's analysis of the act of faith and see how the aesthetic experience can illuminate what it means to believe.

BELIEVING AS AN AESTHETIC ACT

One of Balthasar's chief concerns in his analysis of the act of faith is to overcome a narrow intellectualism according to which faith is primarily a 'believing that'. For Balthasar, faith is not in the first instance an act of the mind. Rather, it is an act of the whole person, an act of surrender of one's whole existence to God in Christ. Hence faith can never be separated from obedience. In terms of the aesthetic categories that we have elaborated above, in the act of faith, Christ impresses his form upon the believer. The subject and the object become so united in the act of faith that the believer becomes Christoformic. Balthasar's analysis undermines the possibility of any dualism from the outset. For our author, the exemplary model of faith is Mary. Recalling the patristic tradition that Mary conceived Christ in her heart by faith before she conceived him in her womb,[9] Balthasar notes that the believer presents God with an active receptivity that is analogous to the woman's active receptivity in accepting the male seed to beget a child. This active receptivity enables the believer to be impressed with Christ's form.

Granted Balthasar's conception of faith as a surrender to the revealing God, we must still go on to ask whether the aesthetic model of faith enables him to avoid shipwreck as he tries to steer a course between the Scylla and Charybdis of fideism and rationalism. In other words, we must ask how aesthetic categories can shed new light on the relation between faith and reason.

The first thing that must be said about the rapport between reason and faith is that the relationship is not conflictual but rather harmonious in that faith and reason complement each other. Here again Balthasar employs the bridal image. Reason gives itself to faith to be fructified. Reason cannot argue its way to faith, but in faith reason comes to its own fulfilment.

Once again Balthasar seeks to avoid dualism and to integrate the subjective and the objective. One classical approach to apologetics has been to stress the objectivity of the historical events and to see them as signs pointing to divine reality. Balthasar wants to preserve the objectivity of the historical moment but he notes the danger of seeing the human mediations as signs pointing to a reality beyond themselves. The other tendency has been to take one's starting point in the subject whose transcendental dynamism leads to the God beyond all categories. Here there is also the danger of a false reduction of faith to mere interiority.

Balthasar's aesthetic approach seeks to overcome this dualism. First, he stresses the reality of the form of Jesus. There is no way to bypass the historical event of God's appearance. But the subject must be led to see what is objectively there to be seen. How does this happen? Balthasar argues that unaided reason itself cannot make the leap. Reason requires the help of God's grace. But what reason can do is to lend in advance a certain credibility to the sign, which makes it possible to see what is objectively visible. Balthasar suggests that we must understand the *praeambula fidei* in a dynamic way.[10] Reason is drawn into faith. As long as reason remains outside the sphere of faith, it cannot see. But once within, there is a genuine seeing.

One of Balthasar's principal theses in his analysis of the act of faith is that seeing and believing are complementary. By believing one is enabled to see and in seeing one believes. The relation between the two is a type of *circumincessio* or mutual indwelling analogous to that which exists between the persons of the Trinity. In proposing this solution, Balthasar alludes to the approach of John Henry Newman (1801–90) and his illative sense whereby from the convergence of the evidence the conclusion results as something suddenly seen.[11] The act of faith is rational in that the data point one in the direction of seeing the form. But the power of synthesis comes not from the subject but from God. In other words, the grace is the light which irradiates from the form drawing the subject to perceive. In this way, the contents of faith and the act of faith form a unity and come together in one aesthetic act whereby in the light radiating from the form the subject sees the form as God in the flesh. One should note that although this act of faith is intensely personal, it is not subjectivistic. On the contrary, what peculiarly characterizes this act is the fact that the subject is drawn out of himself to behold the object of faith. In this sense, Balthasar stresses the extroverted character of the act of faith. The I is expropriated to belong to Christ.

This approach to the act of faith helps us to answer the difficult question of whether faith is an experience. Balthasar notes that for the patristic tradition there was no doubt that faith was an experience, and he observes that if one were to deny this, it is hard to see how one could make sense of the experience of an adult catechumen who at baptism has to profess his faith. The baptism of an adult is the culmination of his initiation into the experience of Christ. The hesitancy as regards experience derives from two factors: first, Luther's accent upon the certitude which the believer experiences in faith, and secondly, the general distrust of the category of feeling when applied to faith.

Balthasar suggests that the solution lies in a closer analysis of what we mean by experience. The German word for experience is *erfahren*, which etymologically suggests the image of a voyage from one place to another. If we look at Paul's experience of faith in Philippians 3, we see something analogous. Paul does not claim to have arrived at the goal. All he knows is that Christ Jesus has made him his own, and therefore, in being conformed to the cross, he hopes to know the power of the resurrection. Thus he presses on, his face firmly turned to the goal. The best image for this experience is that of a flight. Balthasar observes 'Everything is poised in the suspension resulting from having let go of self, in an existence lived in uninterrupted flight toward the goal'.[12] Since Paul's understanding of faith is dynamic and since the goal is only grasped in flight, it follows that faith's destination cannot be translated into a static certainty of salvation. Moreover, if for Paul, faith is surely an experience, it is also an experience whose centre of gravity is away from the self. The whole nature of the experience is the turning away from the self toward the other who is Christ. Here Paul's experience is a confirmation of the paradox of the gospel. To be sure, Paul's experience of faith does not mean that the self is lost. Rather, the paradox consists in the experience that the true self is discovered by turning away from the ego to Christ. Balthasar affirms that faith is an experience, but the experience consists in being taken out of oneself and in being grasped by another. As we saw above, faith is expropriation.

FAITH AND THE SENSORY

One of Balthasar's preoccupations as regards the act of faith is the danger of a false spiritualization. For both philosophical and theological motives, Balthasar argues that the Christian approach to God cannot bypass the senses. First, on the level of anthropology, all knowledge has a sensory base. There is no knowledge which does not involve what the scholastic philosophy of the Middle Ages called *conversio ad phantasma*.[13] But even more decisive is the fact that God in his sovereign freedom has chosen to reveal himself in the incarnation. Thus, our access to God, even in the beatific vision, will always be mediated through the humanity of Jesus.

Obviously a key problem here is the fact of sin which has disrupted the fundamental harmony in which the human person was created. Balthasar notes that Adam before the fall was so interiorly at harmony with God that this interiority radiated outward in such a way that all of creation became a theatre of God's glory. After the fall the process is reversed. God manifests himself in the exterior, in the history of salvation. It is the task of the person to appropriate interiorly what he perceives exteriorly in the history of God with his people.

Christ's incarnation and paschal mystery have won the victory over the disruption caused by sin. Hence it is both possible and necessary that the senses be healed, that the Christian acquire a taste for God which allows him to perceive God present in sensate realities. One of the testimonies that this is possible is Christ's institution of the sacraments. The world exists at Christ's disposal. Thus Christ can, for example, make use of bread to mediate his presence and provide spiritual-sensible food for his people. Even sexuality with its powerful instinctive drives, which can easily lead to egoistic abuse, can be healed and put at the service of Christian love. This is the meaning of Christian marriage. And since faith is ultimately a surrender to the God of love, the God who has given himself for humankind to the point of his self-emptying on the cross, the ultimate test of the authenticity of faith is willingness to spend oneself in love for one's neighbour, the brother or sister for whom Christ died. The neighbour is the sensible experience, *par excellence*, which can never be circumvented in one's pilgrimage to God.

Although Balthasar would argue that faith should lead every Christian toward mysticism in the sense of an ever deeper insertion into the mystery which is Christ, he would equally oppose any attempt to create a dichotomy between the sensory and the mystical.

25

As a son of St Ignatius, Balthasar notes how the author of the *Spiritual Exercises* employs the senses of the exercitant to draw him into the mysteries of the life of Christ. Moreover, in the application of the senses, Ignatius shows how the senses can be integrated into the loving surrender which is prayer. Such use of the senses in prayer should not be considered as a lower and inferior form of prayer to be surpassed by a naked mystical intuition of the divine. The senses, healed by grace, can be already mystical. To be sure, we have already seen that faith is an expropriation, a turning away from the ego, and hence in faith the person will be ready for whatever renunciation God may demand, including the renunciation of all sensible and tangible experience of God. But for the Christian such a renunciation never has the last word. Rather, the renunciation always exists between two moments of vision, the moment when one has really seen the appearance of God in the flesh and the moment of the resurrection of the senses in the *eschaton*.

Another aspect of the pernicious danger of a false spiritualization comes from the temptation of demythologizing. Here we must ask what is the relation of Christ to the world of myth. According to Balthasar, an important turning-point in the history of Western culture was the transition from the world of myth to that of logos.[14] This transition, which is already evident in Plato, marked the rise of the Western philosophical tradition. As Christianity encountered this transition in the form of Neo-Platonism, it met the temptation to believe that ultimately all worldly realities must be left behind in the flight to the One. According to this interpretation, Christ is resolutely opposed to and destroys the world of myth.

Balthasar's approach is rather that Christ integrates the world of myth into himself. Philosophically speaking, we can situate myth within the unveiling of Being in beings. There is no experience of Being, no experience of logos apart from the beings in which Being is revealed. The 'gods' represent unique unveilings of Being to human-kind. The gods are not abstractions but are manifestations of Being in the realm of the finite. When the power of the gods encounters the power of the human imagination, there results the world of myth.

For a Christian, the world of myth is ambiguous. The negative aspect of myth is its understanding of temporality. What takes place in myth happens in primeval time. God, for example, contends with the powers of chaos in an archaic time and overcomes them. God does not really enter into space and time. The radical novelty of the Jewish–Christian faith is that there is a succession of events in which God intervenes in human affairs, thus constituting a history of

26

salvation. The culmination of this involvement is the incarnation and the paschal mystery of Christ.

The positive aspect of myth is that in the face of all rationalistic or mystical attempts to dissolve the finite in the infinite, myth reminds us of the perennial need for the *conversio ad phantasma*. Jesus is the judgement of myth in that he breaks with myth's archaic understanding of time, but he is the fulfilment of myth in that his reality alerts the believer to the necessity of a permanent turning to his earthly fleshly reality in order to behold the invisible God who is beyond the world. Modern proposals for demythologizing faith such as those of Rudolf Bultmann (1884–1976)[15] are really subtle manoeuvres to drive a wedge between faith and history, gnostic efforts to reach the logos by transcending the historical, attempts which ironically end in the very mythological conception of the God–world relationship which they seek to overcome.

THE OBJECTIVE EVIDENCE

Until now we have focused our attention principally if not exclusively on the role of the subject in the act of faith. It is now time to turn our attention to the objective evidence which grounds the act of believing. Here our attention must be directed to Balthasar's analysis of Jesus Christ as the form of Christian revelation.

The first point to be taken into account is the fact of the Christ-event which constitutes the form of our revelational encounter with God. Ultimately this fact and this form can only be understood in terms of the Trinity. Balthasar opposes all attempts to dissect the form. Hence he will not admit any radical discontinuity between the terrestrial Jesus and the Christ proclaimed by the Church.[16] The revelational event of Jesus finds its fulfilment in the faith of the Church. The Easter Jesus is in strict continuity with the pre-paschal Jesus. What distinguishes Jesus from all other founders of religions is the fact that he demands faith in himself as the historical form of the eternal God.[17] Such an act of faith is intelligible only if Jesus is the eternal Son of God. Because Jesus is the eternal Logos, his appearance in space and time has universal significance. Because he is really human, his appearance has the character of an historical event with all its contingency and conditionedness.

As I noted above, Jesus's identity as form must be understood in the light of the Trinity. The Father is the Son's origin and ground. The Son is the manifestation and appearance of the Father. As the scripture says, he is the perfect image of the Father (Col 1:15). The Father impresses his form on the Son. The Son expresses this form to the world. In contrast to non-Christian religions, God is not a formless One. Rather, Jesus as the historical form of revelation makes visible God's trinitarian being as super-form.[18]

The mission of the Son is thus to be the exegesis of the Father. This he can be, because his being as Son consists in his obedience. He always does what is pleasing to the Father (John 8:29). What he sees the Father doing, he does as well. The Son never oversteps the boundary of his mission. Hence, he is the perfect reflection of the Father's being. The Son can only be understood in terms of his trinitarian provenance and trinitarian destiny. At every moment he comes from the Father, not in the sense of the memory of a distant past but of a present actuality. At the same time, in every action he is going back to the Father. His destiny is not only to reveal the Father to the world but to lead believers to participate in his trinitarian being. As Balthasar puts it, 'By his prayer and his suffering, the Son brings his disciples—and through them, all mankind—into the interior space of the Trinity'.[19]

Having considered the fact of the form, we can now turn to analyse some of the qualities of the form. Here too Balthasar appeals to the analogy of the aesthetic experience. First of all, a work of art has its own evidential force and power to convince. If someone fails to appreciate the sculpture of Michelangelo or the music of Mozart, this is more a judgement about him than about the work of art. The same is true of the form of Christ. Christ is his own measure. He cannot be measured by anything outside of himself. To try to do so would already be to destroy the form, for the form claims to be the definitive epiphany of the divine in history. Moreover, if Christ is his own measure, he also claims to be the true measure for the relationship between God and humanity. The right relationship between God and human beings can only be perceived in him. Likewise, just as the beauty of the form of a work of art derives from the harmony of the proportion of the parts, so in the Christ-form we see that all the parts are harmonized around a radiant centre, in this case the relationship of filial obedience of Jesus toward his Father.

At this point, however, it is necessary to confront two thorny problems. First, if Jesus is really situated within the co-ordinates of space and time and really has a human history, how is it that his form is not relativized within the spatio-temporal horizon in which the form appears? In other words, how is it possible to affirm the absolute uniqueness of the form which the form itself demands? Secondly, if the form has its own evidential power, how is it that the form can be misapprehended by so many persons?

As regards the uniqueness of the form, Balthasar first of all expresses his scepticism as to the possibility of classifying the religions according to ideal types. As we saw earlier, for Balthasar the gods represent unique manifestations of Being. Moreover, the whole project of classifying the religions according to types presupposes the so-called suspension of judgement by the perceiver, the famous *epoche* of the phenomenological method,[20] which according to Balthasar renders a true perception of the form impossible. If one tries to stand before the form of Christ in a neutral way without an existential openness to obedience, one will never see the form for what it is. In this way, Balthasar admits that a merely empirical and scientific investigation of the form will never allow a perception of the uniqueness. To perceive the uniqueness of the form one needs the eyes of faith. However, as we saw above, the perception of faith does not contradict reason but rather brings reason to its fulfilment.

Next, Balthasar notes that the form of Jesus involves both a vertical and a horizontal dimension. The form is vertical in that Jesus as the incarnate Son is the one who has descended from heaven. Hence the incarnation means the irruption of the divine in history. But this vertical movement, far from destroying the horizontal, includes it. Jesus is situated within the creation and within the particular history of the Near East and of Israel.

According to Balthasar, one can observe the process of recognizing the uniqueness of the form by looking to the history of Israel. At first, one notices the analogies between Israel's experience and that of other religions. Gradually, however, these similarities fade into the background as Israel's distinctiveness as a religion of promise oriented to a future fulfilment gradually makes itself felt.

The same is true in regard to Jesus. One can note similarities between his mission and that of Old Testament antecedents. These similarities are the parts that make up the form of Jesus. But the form transcends the parts. Gradually, as Jesus' form emerges, his distinctiveness from other bearers of salvation emerges into the foreground. For Balthasar, the heart of his distinctiveness lies in the fact that Jesus demands faith in himself as the revelation of God. Jesus does not point to a way but claims to be the way. Jesus did not undergo a revelation or an enlightenment but possessed the revelation from the beginning. In Jesus, the revelation does not consist so much in what he says or does but rather in what he is, in his person. Ultimately, this leads the believer to grasp his identity as a trinitarian one. He is the Son, the visibility of the Father, his living exegesis.

Finally, we come to the problem of the misapprehension of the form. If the form of revelation has an objective evidence, as Balthasar insists, how is it possible that so many people fail to perceive it? To answer this question, it is useful to recall how Balthasar builds upon the notion of analogy, both the analogy of being and the analogy of beauty. Appropriating the Heideggerian tradition, Balthasar notes that Being remains concealed in the encounter with beings. Being, however, can give itself to be known by unveiling itself. In this moment, Being is lighted up, so that beings reveal the depths of Being which is the source of their being. Hence, the fundamental experience of human being-in-the-world is the experience of the concealedness and the revealedness of Being. Being is both concealed and unveiled in beings. One of the tasks of the artist is to probe the secrets of Being. The artist, through the riches of his anima,[21] is able to overhear the secrets of Being in nature and to bring them to light in a work of art. At the same time, the artist expresses himself in the work of art while concealing himself in it. A true work of art speaks for itself. We can grasp its meaning without knowing the history of the artist or his intention in creating.

Such experiences can help us to answer the question as to the misapprehension of the form. Although Jesus is the visibility of the Father, the form contains a hiddenness which makes possible its misapprehension. First, there is the fact that much of Jesus' life was hidden: thirty years for example at Nazareth and frequent withdrawals from the crowd during his ministry. Then there is the aspect of the silences of Jesus. Moreover, his words, as the words of the eternal Son, contain an infinite profundity. The Holy Spirit must continually open us to their hidden depths. But most important is the astounding fact that Jesus conceals his own identity. Balthasar reflects on this dimension of the life of Jesus in St Mark's gospel and in the fourth gospel. According to Mark, Jesus manifests his identity by his miracles and exorcisms but then commands that his identity be concealed.

St John reflects the same dimension of hiddenness but goes to the root of Jesus' desire to be hidden. John sees that Jesus' hiddenness is itself his revealedness. For John, the self-concealment of the Light is itself a revelation. How are we to interpret this? For Balthasar, the answer lies in the nature of love. If Jesus tries to reveal his identity through signs of power, his reality will inevitably be mis-understood. He will not be understood as love but as power. Since love never does violence, the only way to reveal itself is through self-concealment.

Naturally, here we must introduce an element of supreme impor-tance, the fact of human sinfulness. It is this sinfulness that blinds a person to the true nature of Jesus' identity. Hence from one point of view, the condition for seeing is conversion. But from Jesus' point of view, the condition for a true revelation of his identity is conceal-ment. As Balthasar puts it, when love encounters a sinful world, the only way in which love can reveal itself is through suffering. If divine love wishes to remain loyal to itself without doing violence to a sinful humanity, it becomes suffering. Thus, trinitarian love expresses itself *vis-à-vis* sinful humanity in the cross. Jesus the Lord becomes the servant. The glorification of the Son is not an event subsequent to the cross. Rather, as St John so profoundly grasps, the concealment of the Son under the form of the cross is his glory because it is the manifestation of love to the end. (See, for example, John 12:23–24; 17:1.)

FORM AND FORMLESSNESS

At this point we arrive at the centre of Balthasar's whole theology. We have seen that for Balthasar Jesus is the historical form of the transcendent God. In this sense he is the revelation of supreme beauty. But now we see that for the sake of love the beautiful one descends into the abyss of chaos, hate, ugliness. Hence, Jesus at the end reveals himself as without form. As Isaiah says, 'He had no form or comeliness that we should look at him, and no beauty that we should desire him' (53:2). If this is so, does the project of a theological aesthetics collapse? Are we here led back to the theology of contradiction proposed by Luther, *Deus sub contrario*? Balthasar responds that we are not led to a contradiction but to a paradox. God is not in contradiction with himself, for God cannot deny himself, and it is the nature of God to be love. What the cross reveals is the depths to which God will go to be consistent with himself. On the cross God reveals himself as pure, unbounded love. There is no contradiction here. What the cross reveals is what God's love looks like when it encounters the forces of human rejection. On the cross we see the consistency of love perduring under the condi-tions of hate. Moreover, even the cross invites us to contemplate:

31

'They shall look on him whom they have pierced' (Zech 12:10; John 19:37).

THE DIVINE *CONNUBIUM* [22]

In one of his most memorable poems, 'God's Grandeur', Gerard Manley Hopkins (1844–89) wrote 'The world is charged with the grandeur of God'. One could understand Balthasar's theological aesthetics as an effort to interpret this verse. According to Balthasar, the mythological view of the God–world relationship is that the world is a sacred theophany.[23] Also for the Christian, the world is a theophany of God's glory. But for the Christian the divine beauty cannot be reduced to that of finite forms of beauty and inner-worldly standards of taste. Rather, for the Christian, the theophanous character of the world is revealed in the form of Christ, a form which spans the totality of his life, whose key co-ordinates are incarnation and cross. It is on the cross that we see God's *connubium* with the world. The God of Christians is not a God without passion but a God of divine *eros*. This *eros* leads God to an involvement with his creation. God is a God in search of humankind. This search brings God even to accept catastrophe for himself[24] in order to bring men and women to share in his glory. Thus, on the cross we see that *eros* becomes *agape*, God's searching love is God's self-emptying love. In this sense, as Balthasar says, the cross represents the unity of two unveilings, the unveiling of the sinner to himself and the unveiling of who God is for the world. Thus, a theological aesthetics based upon the form of Jesus contains not only the key to who Jesus is but the key to who the human being is and who God is for humanity. It will be our task in the chapters that now follow to explore these dimensions of Balthasar's thought as we examine his Christology, anthropology and doctrine of God.

Notes

1   See *The Glory of the Lord* 1: *Seeing the Form* (Edinburgh: T. and T. Clark, 1982), pp. 119–20.

2   Ibid., pp. 47–8.

3   A cardinal point in Balthasar's theology is the distinction between an aesthetical theology and a theological aesthetics. An aesthetical theology, which for Balthasar is a negative term, is a theology which takes inner-worldly standards of beauty as the criterion for the beauty

of divine revelation. By contrast, Balthasar envisions a theological aesthetics which lets divine revelation set its own standards of beauty.

4 The doctrine of the analogy of being affirms that there is always some similarity between the creature and God on the basis that the creation proceeds from the creator and must therefore in some sense resemble him.

5 By the analogy of faith Barth meant that the one point where we see the unity between God and his creation is Jesus Christ.

6 Louis Dupré, 'Hans Urs von Balthasar's theology of aesthetic form', *Theological Studies* 49 (1988), p. 309.

7 Balthasar, op. cit., p. 151.

8 Ibid., p. 181.

9 See ibid., p. 539.

10 The *praeambula fidei* are the steps that lead up to faith and help the believer to make the assent of faith.

11 See Balthasar, op. cit., p. 176.

12 See ibid., p. 227.

13 For scholastic philosophy, whatever we know has its origins in sense experience. In knowing, the intellect abstracts the concept from the sensible data through an act of illumination. The intellect always turns to the sensible data in each act of knowing, otherwise its concepts would be blind. In proposing this theory of conceptualization, scholastic thinkers such as Thomas Aquinas are building on the approach to knowing first proposed by Aristotle. See his *De Anima* III, 5 e8.

14 In the history of the human race men and women have always sought the meaning of events and the significance of their human existence. In the period of myth meaning was found through the action of the gods; their intervention in human affairs explained the 'why' of human events. The shift from myth to logos, which is witnessed especially in the rise of Greek philosophy, is the search for the meaning of human life through reason. Plato and Aristotle in differing ways affirmed that reality has a rational structure. This rational structure, which for them had a divine origin, is the meaning of logos.

15 For Bultmann, many of the New Testament affirmations about Jesus are mythological, that is, they presuppose an ancient three-storey view of the universe and try to speak about the God beyond the world in the language of space and time. Clear examples of myth for Bultmann would be nature miracles, resurrection and ascension, the incarnation. He proposes instead an existentialist interpretation of faith which means that God confronts me here and now in the preaching of the gospel and so offers me the possibility of a liberation from an inauthentic life to an authentic one. By authenticity Bultmann intends to say that the person is freed not to cling to his own past but is opened up for God's future. See, for example, Bultmann's *New Testament and Mythology and Other Basic Writings* (Philadelphia, 1984).

16   Some exegetes have maintained that there is no continuity between what Jesus preached and thought about himself and what the Church proclaimed about him. They might say, for example, that Jesus was the eschatological prophet of the Kingdom of God but that there is no basis in the historical Jesus to see him as the incarnation of God. Others such as Bultmann argued that no information about the historical Jesus is necessary for faith, only the mere fact that he existed and died.

17   See Balthasar, op. cit., p. 168.

18   See ibid., pp. 432, 480.

19   Ibid., p. 618.

20   The phenomenologists such as Edmund Husserl (1859–1938) wanted to put a bracket around the existence of the phenomenon under investigation. In this sense they prescinded from the question of truth.

21   Carl Jung (1875–1961) distinguishes between the anima and the animus, the feminine and masculine principle in every human being. The animus is the principle of domination and control. The anima is the principle of creativity. It is the feminine principle of receptivity to the mystery of Being, and lies at the basis of all artistic expression.

22   For Balthasar, the goal of all God's action is union between himself and his creation, a union analogous to the bridal union between husband and wife.

23   The term theophany indicates the manifestation of God. One of the most vivid examples of a theophany in the Old Testament is God's self-manifestation to Moses in the burning bush (see Exodus 3).

24   See Balthasar, op. cit., p. 656.

4

The New Covenant

Balthasar has never developed a systematic Christology. Nevertheless in a number of key essays as well as in the last volume of *The Glory of the Lord* we find in skeleton form the essential elements of a full-fledged Christology. One of the keys to Balthasar's understanding of Jesus is covenant and indeed the last volume of *Glory* bears the title *The New Covenant*.

ISRAEL AS PREPARATION

In Balthasar's opinion the Hebrew scriptures as well as the existence of Israel, taken in themselves, remain an enigma. The idea of promise is central to the existence of the Hebrews. The diverse writings of the Old Testament all point to a future which remains outstanding. It is only in the light of Christ that Israel ceases to be an enigma to itself. Balthasar understands the relationship betweend the Old and the New Covenant to be one of type and fulfilment. The Old Testament is shadow which is brought into the light by Christ. Everything in the Old Testament is *figura* but apart from the revelation of Christ the people of Israel cannot understand their existence as foreshadowing. Balthasar writes 'The essential point is that Israel as a whole and existentially is an image and a figure which cannot interepret itself. It is a sphinx's riddle which cannot be solved without Oedipus.'[1] Only in Christ do the disparate parts of the Old Testament merge into a unity.

When Balthasar reads the Old Testament in the light of Christ, he finds that the experience of Israel pivots around two poles both of which are related to the reality of the covenant. First, there is the idea of God's Word which is not only a word which lets be in creation but also a word of election which creates out of some scattered tribes the people of God. Secondly, there is the figure of the suffering servant. One of the key themes which emerges in Balthasar's theology is that of divine fidelity in the face of sin. How can God remain faithful to himself and to his holiness when his people breaks the covenant of friendship? How can he redeem his people while respecting their liberty? The foreshadowing of the Christological answer is found in the Old Testament figure of the suffering servant. God must bear the sin of his people by entering into their condition of alienation. The way of redemption is the way of suffering.

If the Old Testament is the image and the New Testament the fulfilment, there is no way to pass from the *figura* to the reality except through God's intervention. Only God can create the bridge from the old to the new. Nevertheless there is a person who represents the transition, namely John the Baptist. In John many of the Old Testament themes are recapitulated. He lives in the desert, the place where God wooed his people and made the covenant. He is the prophet who speaks the word of judgement and suffers the martyr's fate. He is Elijah who looks for one to come after him. In Balthasar's words, 'John is the Old Testament transcending itself, the Old Covenant which discovers in the transition the New which is already hidden in it, and precisely by giving itself up, by disappearing and by creating a place for the New is taken over by the New and interpreted by it'.[2] What is important to note here is that the Baptist is totally unable to create the new to which he points. In this he is typical of the entirety of the Old Testament which points beyond itself to a solution which it cannot see. Only in the case of John he does see and bears witness to it. At least, according to the fourth gospel, John is given the clear revelation of Jesus' identity: 'He on whom you see the Spirit descend and remain, this is he' (John 1:33): But John's whole mission is consumed in receiving the revelation and making known the Christ. After this function is fulfilled, he can disappear from the scene.

Jesus, then, is the fulfilment of the promises made to Israel. He is the New Covenant in person. Granted that the reality of the fulfilment exceeds the capacity of our concepts to capture it, we can nevertheless ask if there are some human categories which illumine the mystery of Jesus. Balthasar suggests three: full authority, poverty, abandonment.

JESUS' CLAIM

First, we can note that Balthasar is not interested in some purely scientific search for the historical Jesus. As we have already seen in our study of theological aesthetics, what Balthasar considers important is the recognition of the form which emerges from the New Testament writings. To try to divide the Jesus of history from the Christ of the gospels is already to do violence to the form. Nevertheless, Balthasar observes that it is certainly of interest to note what impression Jesus made on his contemporaries and here we see a striking agreement in all the gospel portraits of Jesus: namely that he acted with a supreme authority which outstripped any of the experiences of authority to which the Jewish people were accustomed. The common impression which we find in the New Testament is that Jesus is incomparably greater than the Old Testament prophets and certainly not to be likened to the religious leaders of his time. As the gospels put it, 'The crowds were astonished at his teaching, for he taught them as one who had authority, and not as their scribes' (Matt 7:28-29).

What are some of the elements that reveal Jesus' overwhelming sense of authority? First, we can note the contrast between John the Baptist and Jesus. The Baptist points to one who will come after him. Jesus does not point to another. He has a sense that in his ministry the fulfilment is already at hand. As he puts it, 'The Kingdom of God is in the midst of you' (Luke 17:21).

One of the striking signs of the presence of the Kingdom is that Jesus is able to restrain the kingdom of Satan through his casting out of demons. Another element is the fact that Jesus' presence brings men and women to a crisis. According to the fourth gospel they must choose between Jesus the light and Satan the power of darkness. But already in the synoptic gospels we find the same basic phenomenon. Our acceptance or rejection of Jesus is the decisive criterion for our admission into or rejection from the Kingdom of God. In the words of Matthew's gospel, 'Everyone who acknowledges me before men, I will also acknowledge before my Father who is in heaven; but whoever denies me before men, I will also deny before my Father who is in heaven' (Matt 10:32-33). This type of text led existentialist theologians such as Bultmann to see faith as the call to decision. But Balthasar points out that it would be more correct to say that Jesus decides about men and women rather than that they decide about him. Even in his mission he claims to be the decisive key to human salvation.

A further aspect of Jesus' authority is attested by Scripture, namely his ability to read human hearts. One can think of the incident where Jesus is invited to dinner by Simon the Pharisee. Simon condemns Jesus in his heart because of Jesus' contact with the sinful woman but Jesus is able to read Simon's judgement. At the last supper Jesus knows that one of his own is about to betray him. Jesus reads the character of Peter and can foresee his weakness in the moment of temptation. In the fourth gospel Jesus is able to read the heart of the Samaritan woman, but throughout the gospels an encounter with Jesus often provokes the awareness of one's sinfulness. One can think of Peter's confession of his sinfulness after the episode of the catch of fish.

Balthasar comments that Jesus' presence makes a man or a woman transparent to himself or herself. By encountering Jesus, the person is brought to a recognition of the true state of affairs. But what is it in Jesus that strips away in others the layers of self-deception? Balthasar suggests that it is Jesus' own transparency to himself. He knows who he is and what mission he has received from the Father. Jesus' complete openness to the Father grounds his sense of authority which provokes the removal of masks by the persons he touches.

Finally, we could note that we get a strong sense of Jesus' claim to authority in the reaction of the Pharisees and high priests who see in his mission nothing less than an incredible arrogance which leads them to conspire to put him to death. All the gospel writers record the incident of the cleansing of the temple and all mention the charge of blasphemy at the trial. Therefore, something extraordinary in the person and ministry of Jesus must have provoked such a hostile reaction. It is clear that the religious leaders saw in Jesus' actions a claim to authority that transgressed upon everything they held sacred in Judaism. In summary, we could say that in this affirmation of full authority we see already a Christological claim of the highest order: Jesus is announcing that he is God's definitive word for the world, a word destined either for the salvation or judgement of God's covenant people and not only for Israel but for all of humankind as well.

JESUS, THE UTTERLY POOR ONE

The second key word which sums up Jesus' existence is the polar opposite of the fullness of authority, namely poverty. Here we can think of the Pauline theme of Jesus' self-emptying. As the Apostle expresses it in 2 Corinthians 8:9, 'You know the grace of our Lord

Jesus Christ, that though he was rich, yet for your sake he became poor, so that by his poverty you might become rich'. Balthasar develops the theme of the poverty of Jesus under three headings: prayer, Spirit, faith.

The gospels, especially St Luke's, portray Jesus as an exemplar of prayer. At the key moments of his life such as the baptism, the transfiguration, the choice of the disciples, Gethsemane, Jesus hands himself over to the Father in prayer. Thus it is no surprise that the disciples ask Jesus to teach them to pray. In response, Jesus teaches them the Our Father, a prayer centred on the Kingdom, which no doubt reflects Jesus' own type of prayer, since his mission was wholly focused on the coming of God's reign. Balthasar notes that this prayer is eminently the prayer of a beggar. The first half of the prayer begs for the future which only God can bring about. It is a prayer of hope that God will sanctify his name, establish his rule and accomplish his saving purposes. This future is wholly beyond the capacity of human power. Man can only beg that God accomplish that which he has promised. The second half of the prayer is more directly focused upon human needs: the need for daily nourishment, the need for forgiveness and finally the desperate need for God's grace to withstand the trial which will precede God's final victory over evil. All these petitions express the poverty of human powerlessness, all ask that God's power be manifest in human impotence.

A second experience of poverty is the need for God's Spirit. In the Old Testament the principal characteristic of God is that God is the living God. God is not like the gods of other religions who are made of silver and gold. One of the chief ways in which the Old Testament expresses the life-giving character of God is through the concept of Spirit. The Spirit is thus naturally associated with God's work of creation in Genesis. According to Psalm 104, when God takes away his Spirit, people no longer have the breath of life and they die. On the other hand, when God sends forth his Spirit, he renews the creation.

All the gospels stress the fact that Jesus is gifted with God's Spirit. He is conceived by the power of the Holy Spirit and receives a new outpouring of the Spirit for his mission at the baptism. According to John, the prophetic word which Jesus preaches is full of the Spirit and hence full of life (John 6:63). But at the same time it would be wrong to say that Jesus possesses the Spirit. Rather Jesus lets himself be possessed by the Spirit. He is open to the inspirations of the Spirit. One of the clear testimonies to this fact is the way Jesus is led by the Spirit into the desert to be tested. Hence we see here a continuing paradox. Jesus is the bearer of the Spirit but he gives the Spirit precisely because he is open to be led by the Spirit. He does not love out of himself, he is power and lives out of the power of the Spirit acting in him. The culmination of this poverty takes place on the cross when Jesus offers himself to the Father 'through the eternal Spirit' (Heb 9:14).

The third characteristic of Jesus' poverty is his faith. Here we find one of Balthasar's more original contributions to Christological discussion, namely his attempt to understand how Jesus is for us the model of faith. First, we can note that Balthasar is breaking with a strong element of the tradition which denied that Jesus possessed the theological virtue of faith because he possessed the beatific vision. Balthasar observes that the only way to overcome the classical position is to return to a more profound and more biblical notion of faith. He believes that part of the difficulty lies in the fact that from Augustine onward theology contented itself with too narrow a definition of faith as a type of non-knowing. In this way faith was contrasted with vision. The two were seen as polar opposites. We already saw in theological aesthetics that for Balthasar faith and vision grow together in a relation of direct proportion. As faith grows, so does vision and vice versa. This would be true even for the saints in the beatific vision. Since God is infinite fullness, there is room for faith to grow infinitely. One can never exhaust the reality of God's richness.

What does faith mean for Balthasar? He points out that the concept of faith in the Old Testament is extremely rich and embraces a number of dimensions. The key idea is that of personal surrender to God, a surrender which involves trust, vigilance, hope, perseverance, waiting, finding refuge. Of course, the priority here is not with man but with God. It is God who in his being is utterly trustworthy and reliable. It is God who has taken a decision in man's regard, and faith is the human response to that decision. Faith is taking one's stance in God's fidelity to himself and to his covenant. In the Old Testament the supreme model of faith is Abraham who trusts in the promise and is even ready to sacrifice his son with a certain blind confidence in the Lord's word of fidelity. The New Testament calls Jesus 'the pioneer and perfecter of our faith' (Heb 12:2). Jesus fulfils the faith of Abraham. His whole life is a surrender to the Father and he entrusts himself to the Father's will even in the darkness of Gethsemane and on the cross. He does not see but he continues to believe.

Here we confront the most difficult aspect of faith, the element of darkness. It is hard to see how one could read the gospels without affirming that Jesus' life embraced an element of darkness which we too experience in faith. Balthasar affirms that there is indeed a darkness yet he would not call it a not-knowing. Jesus knows who he is. He knows that he is the Son. And he knows the Father even in the darkest separation of the cross. But this knowing is not the knowing of the beatific vision. It is the vision of faith where darkness and vision dwell together in harmony. Is this a sheer contradiction? Balthasar says no. The key for resolving the paradox Balthasar finds in love. Love is the absolute reality which grounds Jesus' being. In the realm of love knowledge does not play an absolute role. The lover wishes to know only that which the beloved wishes to reveal. There is no question of a violation of the beloved's secrets. Such is the case between Jesus and his Father. The limits of Jesus' knowledge are his obedience. He only wishes to know what the Father's will is for him. He is satisfied with this knowledge, and for the rest is content to live by faith, to surrender his existence into the Father's hands.

Finally, we could ask what is the relation between Jesus' faith and our faith? We have seen that the New Testament portrays Jesus as the archetype of faith, that is, that Jesus lived the reality of faith *par excellence*. But does this mean that Jesus is merely a model for our faith? Balthasar would say 'no'. The relationship is much deeper. By our baptism we are inserted into Christ. So deep is this insertion that Christ becomes the wellspring and moving force of our existence. As Paul puts it, 'The life I now live in the flesh I live by faith in the Son of God' (Gal 2:20). But in the same verse, he explains further what he means; 'It is no longer I who live, but Christ who lives in me'. Hence, in Balthasar's words, we could say that the mystery of Christian faith consists in the fact that Jesus believes in the depths of my being. Jesus's faith is planted in me so that now I too can surrender myself to the Father. Through baptism my faith is grafted onto his faith as I am incorporated into him. The faith of Jesus and the faith of the Christian become one reality through the union of the believer with the risen Christ.

Before leaving this section on Jesus' poverty, we can note that not only does Jesus live in his own existence a radical poverty before God but in his earthly mission he lives a solidarity with the poor of every type. Obviously, in the first instance, one thinks of the economically poor according to the first beatitude: 'Blessed are you poor, for yours is the Kingdom of God' (Luke 6:20). But Jesus's understanding of the poor is much wider. One thinks of his identification with the simple, with children, with the marginalized such as tax-collectors; lepers; women; the sick; the sinners who represent the lost sheep of the house of Israel. As we shall see later, this identification reaches its culmination in the cross where Jesus becomes perfectly one with every form of God-forsakenness.

SURRENDER

Having seen these two characteristics of Jesus, namely his full authority and his radical poverty, we cannot help but be struck by the fact that these two dimensions seem to be irreconcilable. In his authority Jesus seems to have power over others, in his poverty he appears radically powerless. Balthasar suggests that these two dimensions find their unity in a third attribute which he calls abandonment (*Überlassung*). In other words, Jesus so abandons himself to the Father that his life becomes the perfect expression of the Father's love for the world. Here we arrive at the threshold of the mystery of the incarnation. Naturally no finite creature is ever able to perfectly express the reality of God. God is always the ever-greater one and any analogy of being will be inadequate to express the mystery of the divine. But beyond the analogy of being, there is the analogy of faith, that is, God himself takes the initiative and overcomes the infinite distance between God and man in the Incarnation. Thus Jesus is a fully human reality which expresses perfectly the mystery of God's being. He is, as St John would put it, the *exegesis* of the Father (see John 1:18).[3]

The mystery of Jesus' human existence is that here is a human reality fully at the service of the Father. In his humanity, in his every word and gesture, because of his total surrender to the Father, Jesus can express perfectly the reality of the Father's being. As Balthasar expresses it in a metaphor, his humanity is the keyboard on which the divine music is played.

To return to the theme of glory, the mystery of Jesus' existence is that he can reveal the Father's glory precisely because he does not seek his own glory (John 8:50) and only on this condition can he ask to be glorified (John 17:2, 5). The centre of his existence consists, therefore, in the fact that he does not seek himself. He receives everything in obedience. The supreme symbol for this abandonment in the Johannine theology is the mystery of his hour. In no way does Jesus grasp this hour or seek to force it, he awaits it, as Balthasar would say, with a majestic composure (*majestätische Gelassenheit*).

The difference between Jesus and sinful men and women consists in this: sinful human beings seek to dispose of their lives, to have control of them, to be masters of their reality and even to dispose of God. Jesus, on the other hand, whose life is centred in his surrender to the Father, lets himself be disposed of. He is perfectly at the disposal of the Father but he equally lets himself be disposed of by others.

The hour where Jesus manifests supremely the mystery of his being disposed of is the last supper. He so surrenders himself into the hands of his Father and into the hands of his people that his flesh is given over so that the breaking and distribution of the bread becomes a symbol for the fact that Jesus himself is distributed. He is no longer master of his fate. He lets himself be consumed by the others in a mystery which does not come to an end on Calvary but which continues eucharistically until the end of time. And here too we are at the heart of a paradox. Jesus lets himself be disposed of, but this action is no passivity, for it is in its depths the active handing over of himself for our sakes in love. Thus those in the passion who seem to be the protagonists of the drama turn out to be the ones who are acted upon, for as Jesus says, 'No one takes my life from me, but I lay it down of my own accord' (John 10:18). And yet, Jesus does truly lay down his life and he lets himself be disposed of so radically that his death signifies an abyss between this sinful world and the Father which can be bridged over only by the action of the Father. Thus Jesus' abandonment to the Father is so complete that his life is swallowed up in the omnipotence of death from which only the Father can raise him up. Seen from the human side, the mystery of Jesus' life ends with the enigma of the hiatus. But seen from the divine side, the end of Jesus' earthly existence is not death but resurrection. These events will require further elucidation in a later chapter when we will explore in depth the paschal mystery, but first we must turn our attention to probe in greater detail Balthasar's Christological reflections upon the mystery of the incarnation.

Notes

1 *The Glory of the Lord* 1 (Edinburgh: T. and T. Clark, 1982), p. 628.

2 *Herrlichkeit* III, 2, 2 (Einsiedeln: Johannes, 1969), p. 44.

3 According to this verse, no one has ever seen the Father but the Son has made him known. It is interesting that the verb used in the Greek text is *exēgēsato*.

5

Theology of the incarnation

DESCENT AND ASCENT

Whereas many contemporary authors choose a christological method from below, beginning with the humanity of Jesus, Balthasar unashamedly chooses a method from above. His Christology is based on the Johannine theology of the Word become flesh, and the guiding principle of his reflection could be found in John 3:13 where Jesus says 'No one has ascended into heaven but he who descended from heaven, the Son of Man'. Here we see two leitmotivs in Balthasar's thought: first, the Word descended from heaven, and secondly the Word descended so that men and women can ascend with him. Jesus descends into the flesh so that humanity can be elevated to share his divinity.

The mystery of the incarnation involves the paradox of infinite distance and infinite nearness. The apparent dichotomy between distance and nearness is overcome by the fact that Jesus is the eternal Son and at the same time a man. In becoming human, Jesus does not renounce his identity as Son. Hence Balthasar can talk about the 'where' of Jesus as being with the Father. Whether in his pre-existent state or in the condition of his humanity, Jesus' 'where' is always with the Father. Balthasar writes, 'Whether the Son is in the bosom of the Father or treading the paths of earth, there can be no doubt that the ''where'' that determines his state of life is the mission, the work, the will of the Father. In this ''where'', the Son can always be found, for he is himself the epitome of the paternal mission.'[1]

Already in this quotation we see a number of important dimensions of Christology. First, Jesus knows where he comes from. His origin is from the Father. Everything he sees and does bears witness to the fact that he lives out of this origin. In John 3:11 Jesus says 'I solemnly assure you, we are talking about what we know and we are testifying to what we have seen'. But Balthasar comments that this knowing and seeing does not refer to a pre-existent knowledge or vision. It refers to Jesus' present awareness of his origin.

Secondly, in the quotation we see that Jesus' awareness of his identity is intimately linked to his mission. In Balthasar's thought the uniqueness of the person is always bound to the uniqueness of mission. This is especially true for the Son. His trinitarian identity is intimately bound up with his willingness to undertake the mission of the Father for the salvation of the world.

Finally, we could introduce the theme of obedience. We have already seen that Jesus descends to earth so that men and women can ascend to heaven. But this will only be possible through Jesus' identification with sinful humanity. In the incarnation Jesus takes on our flesh but it is not neutral flesh that Jesus assumes. It is sinful flesh. In Balthasar's vision, the incarnation is intimately linked to the paschal mystery. Jesus becomes man so that he can die for us. Only in this way can we ascend with him. The incarnation is the first step toward Jesus' descent among the dead.

KENOSIS

Sometimes exegetes make a sharp division between the Johannine theology of incarnation and the Pauline theology of *kenosis* (empty-ing).[2] For Balthasar they form a harmonious unity. The Incarnation can only be understood if one presupposes the self-emptying of which St Paul speaks in Philippians 2:5–11. In Balthasar's writings on the *kenosis* he seeks to strike a balance between extreme posi-tions. Perhaps the most important point which he wishes to stress is the divine liberty. God is in no need of the world in order to realize himself. Balthasar resolutely opposes himself to every approach which makes the divine self-emptying a necessity. On the other hand, merely to assert the divine immutability is insufficient, for this truth as such does not do justice to the fact that something really does happen to the Logos in the act of the incarnation.

Balthasar tries to approach the mystery of what takes place in the *kenosis* by saying that it is not the subject who changes but the condition of the subject. The subject remains the eternal Logos. But

45

in the act of the incarnation the divine Logos divests himself of glory and assumes the form of a slave. In the Old Testament, to speak of God's glory is another way of speaking of the manifestation of his power. In an Old Testament context it is unthinkable to conceive of God's glory as revealed in humiliation. But the New Testament doctrine of *kenosis* points to a new understanding of God's being not as infinite power but as infinite love. Each of the persons of the Trinity is a self-emptying in regard to the other persons. The Father does not want to be God without the Son. In turn the Son responds with the gift of his being to the Father. As Balthasar tirelessly repeats, it is impossible to make sense of the Incarnation and of the *kenosis* which it implies apart from the eternal *kenosis* of the three persons of the Trinity. In summary, the *kenosis* of the incarnation challenges us to think God's being anew in the light of love. It drives us to think anew the meaning of transcendence, exaltation, glory. In this context, Balthasar cites a word of Gregory of Nyssa from his catechetical orations:

> The fact that the all-powerful nature was capable of stooping down to the lowliness of the human condition is a greater proof of power than are the miracles, imposing and supernatural though these be ... The humiliation of God shows the superabundance of his power, which is in no way fettered in the midst of conditions contrary to its nature ... The greatness is glimpsed in the lowliness and its exaltation is not thereby reduced.[3]

WHO IS CHRIST?

Balthasar's answer to this question is both simple and classical. He responds according to the classical formula of the Council of Chalcedon, but at the same time his reflection upon the conciliar theology reveals a depth of reflection which requires some explanation. First of all, Balthasar affirms with the Council of Chalcedon that Jesus is the divine person of the Logos. But if we ask: what is Jesus, then we must reply that Jesus is God and Jesus is man. In replying that Jesus is a divine person, Balthasar is siding with the tradition that Jesus is not a human person.

Here a number of points require clarification. First, Balthasar is clear that Jesus is fully human, but he wants to say that Jesus is not a human person. Is this a contradiction? To respond to this question, Balthasar reflects on the meaning of 'person'. As we already noted above, 'person' for Balthasar is intimately linked to mission.

Moreover, every person receives a unique mission from God. Therefore, for Balthasar, personhood always implies uniqueness. In the case of the human person, the person has a spiritual nature which enables him to know and to will. This nature the person shares with other persons. So nature is universal, but person is unrepeatable. However, in the case of the human person, Balthasar argues that person always implies limitation. A human person is limited by space and time, by materiality, by finitude. Jesus too is a person but, being a divine person, his personhood implies no limitation. Hence to deny that Jesus is a human person is to deny that he is limited. This affirmation, therefore, is really the negation of a negation. What at first seems to be a negative affirmation turns out to be the predication of a perfection.

Balthasar is indeed at pains to do justice to the full humanity of Jesus and explains his position in three steps. His first thesis is simply that Jesus is a real man. This means that Jesus is in no way playacting in his humanity. Jesus is the polar opposite of Nietzsche's (1844–1900) superman. Balthasar even refuses to call him a religious genius. Balthasar would have nothing to do with a Schleiermachian type of approach whereby Jesus is different from other men on account of the strength of his God-consciousness. Most important for Balthasar is the fact that the affirmation of Jesus' full humanity implies that, as man, he exists as a creature in infinite distance from God. This truth is the condition of possibility for Jesus' life of faith as we examined it in the last chapter. Without this distance of the creature from God it would be impossible for Jesus to pray. Since Jesus is the archetype of our faith and our prayer and since we are meant to be inserted into his prayer life with the Father, it is essential to maintain the full reality of his humanity. As Adrienne von Speyr expresses it, Jesus must stand as man in adoration before God.

> He must translate the divine distance Father–Son into the Christian distance God–man. And vice versa. In spite of the distance God–man he must in his adoration pray into the nearness of the distance Father–Son. And again he must not live this nearness Father–Son as if he forgot the distance God–man into which he must pray, a distance which on the one hand he must learn but on the other hand a distance which he has so much in himself that in order to learn it he must finally draw it out from himself.[4]

Balthasar's second thesis is that Jesus is real man as assumed man. In other words his humanity is always that of the Logos. Therefore,

47

in his humanity, Jesus always knows himself as Son. As we saw above, this means that Jesus knows his divine origin and he therefore knows himself most clearly in receiving his mission from above. This does not mean that Jesus' self-consciousness consisted of a vision, something objectified, thematic, a religious content that could be made explicit in a specific moment of his life. Rather Jesus knew himself implicitly for what he was, namely the Son, as Balthasar puts it, *interius intimo suo*. Balthasar observes,

> As a man assumed into God, Christ necessarily participates in the self-consciousness of the eternal Son in his eternal procession from the Father and his return to him, and this becomes reflected in the human self-consciousness of Christ to the extent that he experiences this self-consciousness of the Son *interius intimo suo* and that he possesses it by opening himself to it.[5]

Finally, Balthasar proposes the thesis that Jesus is real man *only* as assumed man. Here Balthasar connects Jesus' human experience of God with his life as a member of the Trinity. As we have seen, Jesus' human experience is that of a creature—hence he experiences all the limits and weaknesses of the creature. But this experience of limitation is already the manifestation of the *kenosis* of the act of incarnation and this *kenosis* is rooted in the inner-trinitarian life. We have already noted that all three persons of the Trinity are a self-emptying toward the others. The self-emptying of the Word toward the Father leads him to accept the mission of the self-emptying of the incarnation. Hence Jesus' every experience of creaturely limitation is already the expression of the *kenosis* of his divine being. As Balthasar expresses it, 'The experience of distance from God, which in him constitutes the archetypal *fides*, is as such the expression of God's experience of himself within the Trinity in the distance of distinction between Person and Person'.[6]

In concluding this section, we could note that in Jesus' humanity God finds the man that he intended from the foundation of the world. In this sense Jesus is the new Adam. In Jesus we see that it is possible to live a humanity which is fully autonomous and at the same time fully open to the Father. In Jesus' obedience he expresses perfectly the reality of God. Everything he says and does has the proportion, the harmony which God wants. Hence we see that autonomy and theonomy go together in a perfect synthesis. As the assumed man God takes possession of Jesus but not in such a way that Jesus is passive. Rather he is so possessed that he fully surrenders himself. As Balthasar puts it, 'In this act of taking possession, man is not a merely passive vessel; he is what God has willed him to be: one who responds to the Word, one who corresponds to God's speech. By being dynamically inhabited by God, man is brought to attunement (*Stimmen*) by God: he possesses a voice (*Stimme*), and the right voice at that.'[7] In a word, Jesus' humanity is the perfect correspondence of man to the measure of God.

THEOLOGY OF THE WORD

As Balthasar's theology is highly Johannine in its orientation, it is no surprise that his interpretation of the incarnation is based upon a theology of the Word. Both from the point of view of philosophy, as well as from that of theology, the phenomenon of the Word is extremely rich and thought-provoking. According to Balthasar we can never cease to marvel at the fact that language exists. Indeed it is language which distinguishes the human from the animal. Balthasar notes that language always presupposes three realities: the self-possession of the human subject, freedom, and dialogue between an I and a Thou. No human being ever creates his own language. He receives it as a gift, even though once received, the gift can be infinitely enriched through human creativity. But if no human being as such is able to create the word which makes dialogue possible, how is language possible at all? This question always remains a problem for the philosopher. The human being can only presuppose the word, the bond of communication. In Balthasar's opinion, only a theological answer can resolve the question. Language is possible because man participates in the divine Logos. Language is a gift of the gods.

These reflections have profound anthropological consequences. Man can be defined precisely as one addressed by the word. As Balthasar always insists, the fundamental anthropological reality is the fact of being called into existence by a Thou. Hence he would reject any approach to man which begins with the isolated I or with the thinking subject. Descartes's 'I think, therefore I am' is very much wide of the mark. Rather Balthasar would say 'I am addressed, therefore I am' and this being addressed ultimately means a being addressed by God in love.

But not only is man addressed, he is also summoned to respond and this is indeed what it means to be human. Here Balthasar makes a play on the German word *Wort* (word). The human person is addressed by the word so that he can answer (*ant-worten*). As Balthasar puts in, 'Man is so constituted in his essence that he is endowed with the word to be a response'.[8] This means that it is the nature of man to be in communication, first of all with God and then with other men and women. To miss one's destiny as human being is to fall into a monologue. This is the essence of sin.

Here we can easily link Christology and anthropology. Christ is at one and the same time the address of God to us and the response of humanity to God. He is both *Wort* (word) and *Antwort* (response) in unity. At this point it would be convenient to introduce another factor into our discussion, namely the reality of time. A number of contemporary philosophers such as Rosenzweig (1886–1929) have shown that uttering the word requires time. The word is spoken in history. Jesus as the Word made flesh is the Word uttered in time. Time is one of our most precious gifts, yet it is equally the source of our deepest frustrations. Without time we cannot live, without time we would be incapable of experiencing the deepest human joys. But it is equally true that time marches inexorably ahead. Time cannot be laid hold of. The deepest moments of fulfilment are also transitory. Hence there is a certain tragic quality about time. The present cannot be held and the past cannot be recovered.

But in becoming human, Jesus the Word has lived every moment of time and impregnated this time with the fullness of his divinity. Christ's time is not frustrated time. He received each moment of time from his Father as gift and expressed in that moment the reality of the Word. As we saw in the last chapter in regard to Jesus' hour, he does not seize it or seek to anticipate it. He receives it as gift. Because of the presence of the Word in our history, eternity and time are no longer contradictories. Jesus has shown us that it is possible to redeem the time. Every moment of his time was both a moment of finitude and a moment of the fullness of eternity. Jesus integrated all the moments of human time into his eternity as divine Word.

In Balthasar's book *Man in History* he meditates on the different stages of our Lord's life. Since Jesus lived the various phases of human life and since he has been raised from the dead, each of these stages has in a certain sense become a part of God's eternity and each has a saving significance for the Christian.

The first stage of Jesus' life was that of childhood and this aspect has inspired a spirituality of Christian infancy. One thinks, for example, of Thérèse of Lisieux.[9] A number of features of the child make a striking impression. The child, for example, is radically helpless and defenceless. The child also spends much of his time sleeping. A mother is constantly alert to her child, but she leaves the child undisturbed. This aspect impressed the little Thérèse. She often saw Christ as asleep, seemingly impervious to her needs. But she was content to live by faith and to postpone her requests to later. Another dimension of childhood is playfulness. Adult life is regulated by rules. Children invent their games with creativity and feel free to change the rules to suit their fancy. So in the spiritual life one cannot bind Christ to our rules. We must allow him the seeming caprice of choosing according to his pleasure.

The second phase through which Jesus lived was youth. According to Balthasar it is no accident that Jesus did not grow old, for old age is a period of growing resignation and even of despair. Youth, on the other hand, is a period of fantasy, of seemingly infinite possibilities, of dreams for the future. The Christian who is inserted into Christ is inserted into his youth. How often the New Testament stresses the newness of the man or woman inserted into Christ. A Christian may grow old in body but there is no such thing as the *Christian* experience of growing old. The Christian is called upon ever to be as young as the Lord's resurrection.

Finally, Christ entered into the phase of adulthood. In this stage Balthasar sees the need for decision. The one who is no longer a child but an adult must enter into the seriousness of decision. In adulthood there prevails the seriousness of the deed. All of this is reflected in Christ's summons to the decision of faith. Christ stakes his whole life on the preaching of the Kingdom. So radical is his commitment that he is willing to die rather than renounce his vocation.

At this point it could be useful to recall that all these stages of Christ's life are the stages by which the Word entered fully into time. God's Word to the world unfolded in the untidy sphere of human time. But if Christ is the self-expressive Word of the Father, his life reveals that in the end the Word becomes the deed. God expresses himself in an act of utter self-giving. 'A greater love has no man than this, to lay down his life for his friends' (John 15:13). At the same time we see that the final manifestation of the Word is the non-word of death. The Word of God is reduced to silence and yet Christ remains the expressive word of the Father, for the silence of his death is love poured out to the end. Thus, as we saw in our chapter on theological aesthetics, Christ's death represents both the depths of God's hiddenness and the depths of his revelation. Here once again we see the confirmation of God's manner of acting. As

Balthasar expresses it, 'The deeper God unveils himself, so much more deeply does he hide himself in the human'.[10]

JESUS, THE CONCRETE-UNIVERSAL

One of the problems which has haunted philosophy is how to overcome the apparent dichotomy between the universal and the singular. Every attempt at synthesis seems to founder on the irreducible tension between the two poles which constitute every finite being. Whatever is has an essence which, as such, is universal. The individual being participates in the universality of the essence. At the same time an essence never exists as such but must always be embodied in a concrete singular. Within the realm of our creaturely experience we know that this tension remains irresolvable. Plato sought a resolution in terms of universal ideas participated in by sensible reality. But this approach founders because he seeks a solution on the level of abstract ideas and fails to do justice to concrete existence. In Balthasar's view a breakthrough occurs in Gregory of Nyssa's substitution of the notion of 'totality' for the Platonic idea.

In this context Balthasar argues that only Christian faith finds the solution to the problem posed by philosophy. Jesus as the Logos incarnate is both the Totality (God, Being itself) and the most concrete singular. Only in the mystery of the Incarnation do we find the universal reality of the Totality in the most concrete singular, Jesus of Nazareth. Thus only in the hypostatic union do we arrive at an overcoming of the fundamental conundrum of metaphysics. And here is the scandal of faith. Only in this one, this *concretissimum,* as Balthasar says, do we find the Totality. This man Jesus is God. In Johannine language, 'He who sees me sees the Father' (John 14:9). Thus the stumbling block of Christian faith consists in the fact that there is no bypassing this concrete sensible in our pilgrimage to God. He who bypasses this concrete man will never find the Totality. As Balthasar puts it, for as long as time lasts, the search for God must always turn to this image in a *conversio ad phantasma,* for only in this flesh has the Word become visible and drawn near to us.

Notes

1 *The Christian State of Life* (San Francisco: Ignatius Press, 1983), p. 188.

2 See below, Chapter 9, note 16.

3   Gregory of Nyssa, *Oratio Catechetica* 24 as cited by Balthasar, *Mysterium Paschale* (Edinburgh: T. and T. Clark, 1990), p. 34.

4   Adrienne von Speyr, *Die Welt des Gebetes* (Einsiedeln: Johannes, 1951), p. 75.

5   *The Glory of the Lord* 1 (Edinburgh: T. and T. Clark, 1982), p. 328.

6   Ibid., p. 328.

7   Ibid., p. 475.

8   *Das Ganze im Fragment* (Einsiedeln: Johannes, 1963), p. 255.

9   St Thérèse of Lisieux (1873-97) was a Carmelite nun who within the span of a short life developed a profound spirituality of spiritual infancy.

10 *Verbum Caro* (Einsiedeln: Johannes, 1960), p. 91.

6

The human enigma

INTRODUCTION

Balthasar, as we have seen, does not develop his theology according to traditional dogmatic treatises, and thus it is not surprising that he has not produced a theological anthropology as such. Instead he has chosen to develop his position on humankind within the *Theodrama*. The sphere of drama is the sphere of action. Hence Balthasar is concerned with the divine–human interaction and especially, therefore, with the problem of freedom. The human predicament is that people because of sin have lost the integral freedom which God intended. So people find themselves in a situation where they have some inkling of what they are meant to be and yet are incapable of realizing their destiny. Their situation can be literally described as pathetic. As we shall see later, only God can liberate human beings from their predicament by freely entering into their situation of suffering. The pathos of the human is redeemed by the pathos of the divine. As I have already indicated, men and women know inchoatively that their situation is out of kilter, but they do not know why. This knowledge has been expressed in various cultures and myths. As far back as Plato and the Gnostics, we find the idea of a fall or a fundamental rupture in human existence. But only in Christ is the nature of this division revealed as well as the means toward bringing about healing.

If we had to choose one phrase which would sum up Balthasar's perception of the human situation, I would suggest: humans on the boundary. The human person experiences himself or herself as standing on the dividing line between time and eternity, between the finite and the infinite. People are continually faced with the question of how they can create something of permanent value or eternal worth within the confines of their finitude. How can they encompass the infinite within the boundaries of their finitude? This question pursues them at every turn, they cannot help but pose it. At the same time, they have no means of answering it. In short, they remain an enigma to themselves.

THE PAGAN AND THE CHRISTIAN WORLD-VIEW

One of Balthasar's favourite ways of thinking is to pursue a problem dialectically by contrasting non-Christian and Christian solutions. In this way he can place in relief the dilemma of the human predicament and the tortuous attempts throughout the history of culture to find a solution and at the same time highlight the originality of the Christian position. Such is the strategy which he pursues in regard to anthropology. Here we can develop his thought in three stages: first, the perception of human beings in pagan antiquity; second, the Christian revelation; and finally, post-Christian gropings to find a new vision of the human.

According to Balthasar, if there is any key to the pre-Christian human self-understanding, it is finitude. Especially in the world of Hellenistic thought, the fundamental human wisdom for people consists in knowing their limits. Any attempt to transgress these boundaries results in tragedy.

In addition, Balthasar seeks to describe the vision of the human in pagan antiquity with the term 'hovering analogy'. People stand hovering between the world of nature and God. They live in a world which forms a cosmos, which has a harmony bestowed by the gods. The world as cosmos is already sacred. Human beings have to insert themselves into this sacrality and observe its laws. Balthasar admits that such a vision of reality is difficult for us today and we would be inclined to call it pantheistic but he argues that such a modern term is misleading. The truth is that the human beings of antiquity were aware of living in a sacred world where they hovered between nature and God.

This sacred vision of the universe was already broken with Pythagoras (c. 570–c. 500 BC) and his idea that 'man is the measure of all things'. Once this view is accepted, the human is no longer a microcosm of the sacred universe and the harmony of the cosmos is shattered. But the unity was dissolved once and forever with the revelation of the Creator God of the Old Testament. With this revelation the sacred cosmos of antiquity was definitively abolished. No longer would it be possible for people to seek security in the womb of an all-embracing mother nature. Rather they were summoned from this sacred womb to the liberty of being God's covenant partners. For over two thousand years this vision of their destiny gave to the human creatures a sense of meaning amidst all the vicissitudes of their precarious existence. The plight of post-Christian people is that they are robbed of this sense of destiny and yet are unable to re-establish the sacred harmony of pagan antiquity. Hence they are left with the burden of carrying their own freedom which now has a weight they are unable to carry. Having been thrown into a world which is no longer sacred and having had thrust upon them the inescapable burden of freedom, they cannot help but live a daily alienation. Hence human existence is lived as an enigma from which only Christ can deliver it.

DIMENSIONS OF THE HUMAN ENIGMA

Within this perspective of the dialectic between the humanism of antiquity and the Christian vision of the human, we can unfold Balthasar's portrayal of the human enigma in a series of irresolvable tensions which can only find their resolution in the God-man.

The first tension is that between matter and spirit. We noted at the beginning of this chapter that humankind stands on the border between the finite and the infinite. In other words, we human beings stand at the mid-point between the world and God. On the one hand, men and women belong radically to this world and have their roots in the earth. Without the material substructure of human existence the human being could not survive. But it is equally true that human beings do not live by bread alone. For from the earth they reach out to God. Speaking philosophically, we could say that it is the nature of human beings to transcend themselves in freedom toward God. Or, as the existentialists would say, it is the human essence alone which is without an essence. The human horizon is unlimited. It opens out to the divine.

We can readily see that here human beings live a tension which admits of no final solution, and the temptation to reductionism exists from both sides. On the one hand, they can suppress the material dimension and opt for a one-sided spiritual vision such as that proposed by Neo-Platonism or Buddhism. On the other hand, they can sink back into their animal origins and live only for the gratification of their instincts. But neither approach resolves the dilemma. The Christian response will be in terms of the incarnation. God redeems matter by immersing himself in it through the incarnation. Jesus lived human material existence to the full and summoned it to the destiny of resurrection with him. One of Balthasar's favourite words is 'bodiliness'. No flight from the world is permitted to a Christian. Christ became flesh in the incarnation and the permanent sign of the value of matter is the bodiliness of Christ offered to his people in the eucharist.

The next irresolvable tension of the human is found in sexuality. Balthasar is fond of reminding us that we are sexual to the depths of our beings. Every dimension of human being is characterized by either femaleness or maleness. One's identity is expressed in one's sexuality and yet one always experiences one's identity as an incompleteness. One longs for the other sex to find fulfilment. But this union is never completely realizable. Although sexual union is possible, the union is always fragmentary. This is due in part to the fact of materiality discussed above. In spite of sexual union the two persons will remain separate bodies. But the deeper reason for imperfect union lies in the freedom of the other which remains always beyond my control.

From the religious perspective Balthasar notes that sexuality has always played a key role in the great religious traditions. But here again the tendency is to opt for a one-sided solution. One can with antiquity deify sexuality and attribute sexuality to the gods, thus capturing them within the sphere of the finite, or one can seek to expel sexuality from the human and from the religious as in Manichaeanism.[1] The biblical view seeks to preserve the balance by maintaining on the one hand that God is transcendent and so beyond sexuality, and by defending on the other hand the goodness of human sexual relations since these form part of a good creation willed by God.

Before saying a word on Christ's relation to sexuality, it would be useful to add a word on another aspect of sexuality which heightens its tension-filled character, namely its relation to death. Sexuality as the primordial expression of our materiality is essentially linked to our finitude and hence to our death. Modern psychology since Freud (1856–1939) has made us aware of the link between love and death and has pointed out how every orgasm is itself a foreshadowing of death. But almost two hundred years ago the philosopher Hegel meditated upon the relationship between sexuality and death and pointed out that propagation is already the response of the human species to the problem of death and argued that since individuals feel inadequate, they seek to overcome their isolation by propagating themselves and losing themselves in the species. Thus Balthasar points to the ironical fact that the existence of marriage is a constant reminder of death.

As with the tension between matter and spirit, so with sexuality there is no resolution of this enigma of the human spirit apart from Christ. The coming of Christ was inextricably bound up with sexuality in that his birth is inserted into the history of a particular people, namely the Hebrews. But at the same time his conception from a virgin was the first step in overcoming the vicious circle between sexuality and death. The whole life of Christ was in turn a self-giving. But Jesus never surrendered himself bodily to a woman. Such a surrender would have compromised the mission he received from his Father. For Jesus was summoned not to give his life to one person but to all men and women. This is the meaning of his death as well as the meaning of the Eucharist which flows from it. In giving his life for all, Jesus fulfilled the promises of the Old Covenant and opened up the possibility not only of Christian marriage but also of Christian virginity. The man or woman in Christ no longer has to fear death, for he or she is called to the resurrection of the flesh. Since sexuality has been liberated from death, the Christian is free to choose a different kind of fruitfulness, the spiritual fruitfulness of virginity while leaving it to God to scatter the seeds of this renunciation of genitality to bear fruit according to his providence.

A third tension which points to the enigma of the human situation is that between the individual and the community. In the world of antiquity the accent lay upon the communal dimension, upon the *polis*. An individual found his or her meaning and identity by being inserted into the political community. But the *polis* was not just a sociological reality. The *polis* was itself an embodiment of the divine character of the cosmos. In this context the laws of the *polis* themselves expressed the sacred character of existence. Something similar existed in Israel. The individual Jew found his or her identity by being part of God's covenant people.

At the same time the community can never absorb the individual precisely because every human being is a person. It was Christianity that underlined for the first time in such a radical way the transcendent value of the person. Each individual has infinite value, for he or she is called by name in Christ. Thus, the Christian interpretation of human beings in society envisions a dialectical tension according to which the individual exists for the community but the community exists for the person—an idea that was developed by Jacques Maritain.[2]

Here, in Balthasar's words, the key to understanding the reality of the human is to be found in the Mystical Body of Christ. The Christian lives out the communal dimension of existence by being inserted into the Body of Christ, the *communio sanctorum*. Each member of the Body lives with and for the others. So deep is the reality of the Body that one member of the Body can always pray for the others as well as suffer for them. It is the conviction of faith that no prayer ever goes unheard. Its fruitfulness will be felt somewhere in the Body. At the same time no suffering is ever useless and indeed some Christians will be invited by Christ to suffer vicariously for other members. Nonetheless, although each member exists only within the Body, he or she is not submerged in a collectivity. Each person has a direct relationship with Christ the Head and the unique identity of each is expressed in the mission he or she receives. There is no Christian who has not received a unique, personal, irreplaceable sending by Christ.

Before leaving the problem of the tension between the individual and the community, we ought to mention another phenomenon, so primordial and important for human existence, which highlights this polarity. I am referring to the phenomenon of human language. Language refers not only to words but to the whole range of human communication expressed in signs and symbols. Language is always a phenomenon of community. In Balthasar's view, children first become aware of themselves through the smile of their mother. Gradually they learn to speak, and the language they use is the gift of the community to them. No one on his or her own ever invents language. Yet once language is given, the individual can modify it with almost infinite creativity. Balthasar would argue that language is a mystery which philosophy as such can never fully fathom. If no individual as such can ever invent language, how explain the fact of its existence? Balthasar would argue that no empirical explanation will ever do justice to the *human* phenomenon of language. Ultimately the fact of language points to the reality of Logos which binds persons together and makes human communication possible. In other words, the fact of language points to a religious origin. Human language takes place because humankind has its roots in the transcendent reality of Logos whose historical name is Jesus Christ.

THE SPHINX OF DEATH

We began this chapter by describing the human situation as life on the boundary. The fundamental enigma for men and women is how to create something definitive and eternally valuable within the sphere of the finite. In saying this we are already touching upon the mystery of death, for it is precisely death which is the concrete manifestation of finitude, and it is death which irretrievably shatters every human attempt to create something definitively and finally lasting.

In a certain sense the entire history of culture can be seen as human attempts to come to terms with death. Balthasar mentions three ways in which human beings have sought a solution to the inevitability of death. The first is *eros* which seeks to affirm the eternal value of the beloved other. Many poets and philosophers have pointed out how the reality of human love is an implicit affirmation of immortality. As Gabriel Marcel (1889–1976) expresses it, every time one loves another person, one says implicitly: you shall never die. The poets as well have shown that every act of love is a groping for eternity. In the act of love one experiences an intimation of immortality which one hopes will never pass away. Yet there is the contradiction between the hope one experiences and the stark reality of the death of the beloved.

A second attempt to come to terms with death is the exercise of power. One seeks to overcome one's finitude by power over others, by creating monuments for oneself which overcome the perishability of death. One thinks of the tyrants who have been the landmarks of human history such as Alexander the Great, Julius Caesar, Charlemagne, Napoleon, Hitler, Ceauşescu and the like. Yet all such attempts to build universal kingdoms and thousand-year reigns have inevitably crumbled in the dust of war and cultural decay.

Finally, Balthasar mentions art as a protest against death and notes as well how much of art is linked to the struggles for power. Our museums consist nearly always, at least in part, of the spoils of war.

We noted above that one fundamental tension between finitude and infinity was expressed in the dialectic between the individual and the community. This dialectic, Balthasar observes, is strongly manifested in the mystery of death. It is a truism to say that everyone dies alone. I can be surrounded by others but in the end death expresses the mystery of my being which no one can take from me. There is nothing which is more radically mine than my death.

Balthasar points out, with his great love for dramatic literature, that even in the great death scenes of lovers such as Antony and Cleopatra, Tristan and Isolde, Romeo and Juliet, there is no simultaneity in death. Even the mutual death of lovers cannot overcome the solitude of death.

Yet it would be mistaken to say that death is merely an individual affair. On the one hand, there is clear testimony that it is possible to give one's life for another. One thinks, for example, of the great martyrs such as Maximilian Kolbe (1894–1941).[3] But even on the more pedestrian level, parents must think of providing for their children as they prepare for death, and psychologists such as Erickson[4] have shown that part of maturity consists in passing on the best of what one has and is to future generations. Thus it turns out that even the reality of death always has a communal dimension. Here too we see a dialectic which admits of no unilateral reduction.

I have spoken of the sphinx of death. With this term I would like to indicate that all human attempts to solve the riddle of death have remained failures. Balthasar enumerates at least five. First, there is the naturalistic explanation that death is merely a return to the earth from which one came. One returns to mother earth. But is this any longer accessible to us after the desacralization of the cosmos with the coming of the Hebrew faith in the Creator God? Then, there is the way of the Eastern religions. For these religions death is not important, for one loses one's individuality in Nirvana. The solution to the problem of death consists in the surrender of the ego. But here has not one surrendered one pole of the tension between individuality and community by dissolving individuality in the faceless mass of non-Being? A similar approach is the transmigration of souls which in its turn denies its starting point in the reality of the individual and which does not take seriously the significance of finite freedom.

Then there is the Jewish approach which too puts its accent upon the communal pole, seeking to preserve the pole of the value of individuals by immersing them in the reality of the covenant people. For Jewish hope it is enough to have lived for a brief time under the sun of the God of the covenant. One may then die in peace hoping for the realization of God's promises in the coming messiah. But already in intertestamental Judaism the excessive strain of this approach was felt with the overwhelming force of the suffering of the Jewish martyrs and the apparent triumph of evil over God's covenant love. Thus Judaism first grasped in anticipation the Christian vision of the resurrection of the dead.

Finally, one could mention the solution of Stoicism, the heroic despair which has been announced by philosophers from Seneca (*c.* 4 BC–AD 65) to Heidegger. The human being is a being-toward-death and the best one can do is acknowledge the situation and take responsibility for one's death in an act of unflinching self-acceptance and self-determination.

All these approaches reveal that death remains a riddle and that the human situation is an enigma. At times there are moments of light in the darkness, human acts such as hope, selfless love, unshakeable trust, forgiveness where justice would have sufficed, which point in an oblique way to the Light who is Christ. But, in Balthasar's opinion, the best word to describe the human situation apart from the light of Christ's revelation is longing or desire (*Sehnsucht*). One longs for the light, longs for meaning, for final validity and value. One somehow knows that such a light must exist. In fact one's questioning presupposes the light, and yet apart from Christ's revelation, the light remains veiled in shadows. Face to face with the inevitability of death, one pounds on the door of fate but the gates of Hades remain closed until Christ opens them in his resurrection. Balthasar suggests that perhaps the most apt word available to sum up this situation would be the Kantian term 'postulate'.[5] I do not *know* that there is final meaning, eternal value, immortality, and yet my human existence drives me to postulate all of these because otherwise human life would be intolerable. Nevertheless, a postulate remains a postulate and not a given.

The postulate character of human existence reminds us that in the end there is no resolution of the human enigma from below. Humankind can and must search and seek but the answer must come from above, from Christ, as gift. All attempts at grasping, all clutching at answers are bound to fail. Only in the recognition of one's poverty are the doors of Hades thrown open and humankind is offered gratuitously the grace of eternal life which remains sheer undeserved gift.

CHRIST, THE RESOLUTION OF THE ENIGMA

In this concluding section of the chapter we can repeat in summary the main thesis which we have seen in this section, namely that Christ is God's answer to the enigma of the human. The key is the mystery of the incarnation. If human beings live on the boundary of the finite and the infinite, Jesus Christ lives on both sides of the boundary. As eternal Logos he is infinite God but as incarnate Logos he has taken upon himself the reality of our finite existence.

The phenomenology of the human which we saw above revealed that men and women live a series of tensions which do not admit of resolution. Indeed these tensions are so great that, even apart from faith, philosophers and poets have spoken of a fall or of a rupture in human existence. Somehow human life is experienced as a division which should not be. But Christ's coming has revealed two truths. First, it is possible to live in an authentic and integrated way the tensions of human existence. If human life is a tension, how much more the tension of the God-man. Balthasar speaks of the reality of the incarnate life of Jesus as a hypertension (*Überspannung*). Yet within this heightened tension every gesture, word and deed of Jesus revealed the pattern of the human as God intended it.

Moreover, Jesus not only lived the tensions of human existence. He also embraced the riddle of death. Balthasar points out that only Christianity has given a redemptive significance to death itself. Other religions and philosophers have perhaps pointed to a way of circumventing death. One can think here of solutions such as those proposed by Stoicism, Gnosticism and Buddhism. But Jesus alone plunges to the depths of death and in the midst of death opens the way to resurrection. The Christian thus does not seek to circumvent death. Rather death itself becomes the means to salvation. As Paul says, 'We are treated as dying, and behold we live' (2 Cor 6:9).

In a later chapter we must look more closely at how Christ's death becomes saving for us, at how the death of one brings redemption for many. But here it can be sufficient to conclude by observing that in the end the solution to the human enigma, an enigma so great as to be intuited as a rupture dividing men and women from their deepest selves, is given only by an event outside of themselves, the redemptive death of Christ. Balthasar drives home this point by a wordplay on the two German words for solution and redemption. The *Lösung* (solution) of the human enigma is to be found in no other way than through *Erlösung* (redemption), that is, through the free vicarious self-offering of Christ for the liberation of humankind. It will be the task of the next chapter to explore in more detail the meaning of liberty in order to prepare the stage for understanding the drama of redemption as the interaction of two freedoms, the divine and the human.

Notes

1 Manichaeanism is a system of belief which infiltrated the Christian community in the patristic era. The system was based on a dualism between two opposing principles of light and darkness. The cosmos is in thrall to the principle of darkness. Matter is intrinsically evil and human beings are summoned to be liberated from it. Hence sexual relations in this system are regarded as evil.

2 Jacques Maritain (1882–1973) was a French Thomistic philosopher especially noted for his attempt to apply Thomistic philosophy to political and social questions.

3 Maximilian Kolbe was a Polish Franciscan priest who freely offered his life in place of a father of a family in the concentration camp of Auschwitz.

4 E. H. Erickson is a contemporary developmental psychologist who has revised the Freudian position on development and has shown that human development does not cease with the end of childhood but continues into adulthood and even to old age.

5 In Kant's philosophical works he said that he wanted to do away with knowledge to make room for faith. According to his doctrine it is impossible for one to know the realities of God, freedom and immortality. But one must postulate their existence in order to make the reality of the moral life intelligible.

7

Divine and human freedom

INTRODUCTION

The whole of the biblical revelation rests on the fact that God has freely created us and has graciously intervened in our history to make us his covenant people and to redeem us in Christ after we had fallen into sin. In other words, without the presupposition of a God who is infinitely free in his love, the biblical revelation collapses. After two thousand years of Christianity, the presupposition of a free God is often taken for granted. Yet we often forget that the affirmation of the freedom of the Infinite was one of the startling novelties of biblical revelation.

Hence at the beginning of Balthasar's treatment of the question of divine and human freedom he puts us on the alert to a number of positions which exclude the possibility of a solution from the beginning. The first is the Neo-Platonic doctrine of Plotinus (c. 205–270) according to which the One means infinite fullness and infinite freedom in itself, but a freedom which is basically closed-in upon itself. The One of Plotinus is not free to enter into relation with that which is other. The Neo-Platonic doctrine of the One excludes a genuine rapport between the One and the many. Plotinus's God is ultimately a metaphysical egoist.

A more modern approach to freedom which equally leads to a cul-de-sac is that of Hegel. Hegel's Absolute arrives to self-consciousness by setting up an opposition with another and by returning to self through that other. In this philosophical vision the world is a necessary moment of the divine realization of self-consciousness. God is not free in himself but is only free through the other. Here there is no dramatic relationship between God and the world.

Ultimately, the approach which Balthasar takes to the divine freedom rests upon the trinitarian nature of God. Because God is Being as such, we cannot speak of any 'outside' of God. Does this reduce the world to an illusion? If there is nothing besides God, where do we place the world? First, Balthasar affirms that we must think of the world as inside God. The place of the world is the infinite space between the divine persons.

Secondly, Balthasar appeals to Nicholas of Cusa's (1401–64) doctrine that God is the totally Other precisely as the Not-Other. God is the totally Other in the sense that he is the creator and transcendent source of our being. There can be no confusion between our being and God's Being, for in every dimension of our being we are dependent upon and receptive of God's creative and preserving activity in order to exist. But at the same time God is not other, for we are wholly in him. We receive our being from him. We come from God and we belong to him. As St Paul expresses it, 'In him we live and move and have our being' (Acts 17:28).

Some faint perception of what this means can be grasped by looking at the Trinity. There too God is three times different (*alius*) in the sense that each of the persons of the Trinity is not the other persons. But at the same time God is not three times different from himself (*aliud*). God remains the same in his nature. Hence the Trinity brings us face to face with the mystery that there is a real otherness in God which is not incompatible with his unity. Hence the Neo-Platonic monadic conception of God is shattered once and for all by the Christian revelation of the Trinity. Oneness is not incompatible with otherness. Thus it is not surprising that the triune God can make room for the otherness of the creature. Creation must, in the last analysis, be understood in a trinitarian way. Since God is Trinity, he does not need the creature, for his love is already realized in the infinite perichoresis of the three divine persons.[1] At the same time, the three persons share, so to say, an infinite space of reciprocal giving, exchange, initiative and response. The divine persons have freely chosen to share their love by creating and have inserted creatures into this infinite open space of their divine life.

This conception of the divine life as the infinite free self-giving of the persons thus makes possible the reality of a free creation as well as the interchange of freedom in the divine drama between God and the world. The goal of God's free dramatic action is, in Balthasar's judgement, the setting free of the creature. In the action of creation God first of all enables an autonomous creature to be. He lets it be and hence be free in its very being. Later, after sin, the trinitarian love confronts the creature enslaved by its misappropriation of freedom, and in turn sets it free for the purpose envisaged by the Trinity from eternity, namely the liberty of sonship in Christ.

To develop these schematic ideas now in more detail, let us look in turn at both sides of the divine–human encounter, first at the reality of the creature and his finite freedom and then at the reality of the Trinity with its infinite freedom.

THE MYSTERY OF FINITE FREEDOM

Let us begin with a reflection upon self-consciousness. The essential point which distinguishes a human being from all other creatures of our world is the fact that the human person can say I. Involved in this ability to say I is the fact that persons are aware of themselves. Moreover, my I is unique to me. It is what makes me radically myself and distinguishes me from all other things and persons. There is nothing more radically my own than my subjectivity.

However, it would be wrong to assume that what is most my own isolates me from the world or from others. For it is equally true that my I is a gift which I first receive from another. As we have already seen, I first become aware of myself in the smile of my mother. My I is called into being by the love of another.

This fact reveals the truth that human self-consciousness is always bi-polar. At one and the same time I am aware of myself and I am aware of the other. I belong to myself by belonging at the same time to what is beyond myself; in fact, the I opens out in extension to all reality so that it is possible to say that I belong to myself by belonging to being as such. As St Thomas Aquinas (c. 1225–74) affirmed, the human knower is in a certain sense all things, for human consciousness opens out to the totality of being.

What we have said about self-consciousness can be developed along similar lines for the mystery of freedom. Here too we see two dimensions. The first is that of autonomy. All human beings aware of themselves not only know themselves but also posit themselves. They will themselves to be. They are free to be themselves and to take responsibility for their destiny. Balthasar wants to take human autonomy with radical seriousness and in this connection applies to the human person the phrase of Gregory of Nyssa: human being is *autoexousios*, that is, able to be from itself.

But if we stressed only the pole of self-possession, we would fall into a reductionism. For autonomy is balanced by movement beyond self toward the other. If one tried to have autonomy without movement beyond self, one would be stultified. One would atrophy and die of starvation.

Hence we see that finite freedom consists of a balance of opposites. Finite freedom is autonomous but its autonomy consists precisely in its movement. And since the movement of freedom opens out to the infinite, every achievement of freedom, every experience of autonomy, will itself lead to a new movement toward the God who is ever greater and can never be mastered. As Balthasar puts it, the experience of the fulfilment of freedom and the corresponding experience of the ever-increasing longing for freedom grow in direct proportion.

But since freedom is a search for the Infinite, since human freedom is hungry and in need of Infinite Fullness, does this mean that ultimately the search for God is an egoistic search for self-fulfilment? Here Balthasar follows the approach of St Thomas. The movement of freedom is a movement toward the Good as such and naturally this Good is also the Good for me, that in which my being finds its goal. But the goal of freedom is not only the Good. It is also the True. In other words, the Good is good for me because it is in itself true. There is a mutual indwelling of the Good and the True. Since the Good is also the True, it has value in itself. It must be affirmed as worthy of recognition. The Good is sought not only as good for me but also as good in itself.

As we have seen in this section, the self only exists in relation to the Totality of Being. There is no I apart from its belonging to Being. Hence the paradox of human freedom is this: I can only love myself by loving God. For at the depths of my being I find God to whom I belong. Self-love is impossible without love of the other.

Thus far our analysis of finite freedom has proceeded along philosophical lines. But at this point Balthasar demonstrates how the philosophical analysis arrives at an aporia.[2] On the one hand, as we have seen, freedom is both self-possession and movement toward the Infinite. What is the term of this movement? What is the ground of our self-possession? The answer would seem to be God himself or Being itself. In other words, the term of human freedom is that ground of freedom which is no longer in movement but which is its own source of being. We could call this Ground of Being self-subsistent being, being in and for itself, absolute self-possession.

But, at the same time, in our experience we never experience this Ground of Being except in beings. We never know God in himself. Our experience of God is always mediated through creatures. Thus, from a human point of view, it seems that Being is not self-subsistent. Rather Being dwells in beings and is known through beings. The Ground of Being reveals itself in the beings.

These two aspects of our experience seem to lead us to a contradiction. On the one hand, Being is the self-subsistent ground of our being. On the other hand, we never experience Being on its own but only in beings. Thus the dilemma: is God really absolute freedom or does God exist only in creatures?

Before this dilemma human philosophies and the great religious traditions have sought to give an answer. The atheist says that there is no ground of freedom beyond finite freedom. Human beings are their own ground of freedom. The Buddhist affirms that Being is not self-presence nor freedom. Hence finite freedom should relate itself to Being by dissolving itself in Nothingness. For the Buddhist freedom is ultimately an illusion. Being and Nothingness coincide. Only Christianity dares to affirm that God is infinite freedom. God is infinite self-possession in himself, the fullness of trinitarian love, and God reveals himself in beings precisely through the mystery of creation.

The great philosophical question: why is there being and not nothing requires the light of revelation for its answer. The great ontological difference between Being and beings finds its ultimate illumination through the biblical revelation of the fact of creation. God is self-subsistent freedom, but God chooses to share his freedom with that which is not God. Thus finite freedom turns out to be a primordial giftedness. Paradoxically my autonomy is bestowed autonomy. And thus the fundamental attitude of the free creature before God can only be that of thanksgiving. Christianity reveals the meaning of freedom to be eucharist.

THE MYSTERY OF INFINITE FREEDOM

As we have seen, the great gift of Christianity to humanity consisted in its proclamation of the infinite freedom of God. And this means not only God's freedom in himself but also his freedom to go out of himself and bestow himself on creatures. Moreover, the mystery of divine freedom coincides with the mystery of the Trinity. Here

Balthasar wishes to develop a dynamic conception of the divine trinitarian life which avoids two extremes.

First, Balthasar rejects the idea of God as a rigid, static absolute. Secondly, he rejects an idea common in process philosophy and theology[3] that God can grow in his relation to the world. Creatures cannot add anything to God's Being since God is already infinite fullness. This is the element of truth in the classical conception of divine immutability. But neither is it true that God's essence is static. There is a dynamism in God which admits of infinite variety, vitality, élan and even novelty. When Balthasar begins to describe the divine life, he generally uses poetic, symbolic language and we can see that here the capacity of language to express the mystery of the divine fecundity reaches its limits.[4]

Balthasar attempts to describe the vitality and movement of the divine life through a series of contrasts. On the one hand, God is infinite self-possession. But this self-possession is balanced by total self-gift. None of the divine persons keeps his divinity for himself but rather each gives himself to the other persons. Thus, we could also say, each of the persons is characterized by an infinite 'having' but their having is at the same time their self-donation. Finally, possessing the fullness of the divine life, the three persons are infinitely rich but they are equally poor, for they do not want to keep their divinity for themselves but rather desire to give it away.

Balthasar uses other poetic expressions to try to capture the mystery of the Trinity. He speaks of infinite spaces of play, of the element of surprise, of ever new inventiveness in the quality of their love and even of a dynamism of requesting and responding.

With this background we can say a word about the relation of the Trinity to the world. We have already noted that the world has its place within the Trinity. Moreover, Balthasar links the existence of the world to the three persons. Obviously, the Father is the origin of all self-giving and hence is the origin of the divine project of creation. The Son is the archetype of the world. The Logos is the realm of the divine ideas. What each thing is meant to be is already contained in the infinite Word. This is most especially true for the human being who is made in the image of God, that is, is called to the likeness of the Son. But the Holy Spirit also plays a decisive role in the act of creation, for the Spirit can be described as the ecstasy of God. It is the Spirit who opens the love of the Father and Son outward to the creation.

Next we can note that Balthasar shows how the affirmation of God's freedom avoids two false interpretations of God's relation to the world, namely that of necessity and that of chance. The world would be necessary to God if he could not exist without it. One could ask whether philosophical theism does not tend in this direction, since a monadic God would need some other to relate to, especially if one wants to affirm that God is love. But the trinitarian God is already eternal community and hence does not need the world to be love. It would also seem that the God–world relationship as proposed in pre-Christian antiquity offered a form of necessity *vis-à-vis* the world's relationship to God. For in this perspective God's transcendence is not stressed. Rather God is thought of as the depth dimension of what is. Finally, in this vision it is impossible to separate the divine from the creaturely element. God is the abiding substance underlying the changing flux of finite reality.

With the introduction of an infinite free God by Christianity, the opposite danger emerged, namely of seeing the world as mere chance. There is no reason for the world's being, hence creation and redemption are reduced to the arbitrary decision of God. This version of divine freedom appeared in late mediaeval nominalism[5] and in part was responsible for the terror which Luther felt before the holy majesty of God. If God is capricious, how can I have any certainty about his purposes for the world? What security do I have before my overwhelming need of salvation? In part, the problem of voluntarism[6] resulted from a disastrous separation of the divine knowing and willing, between the divine truth and goodness. In reality God's knowing is rooted in his truth. Moreover, for the Bible, God's relation to the world can be expressed in the word fidelity. God is faithful to his saving purposes, for God is faithful to himself (see 2 Tim 2:13). God's freedom and God's fidelity go hand in hand. From the human point of view, the response to God's fidelity and freedom is trust. By surrendering oneself to God's loving purposes, one finds the sure foundation for one's existence, a foundation which can never be shaken, for it is rooted in God's fidelity.

If God's relation to the world is neither that of chance nor of necessity, then, in Balthasar's language, God sets the world and the creature free to be themselves. God's freedom is in no way in contradiction to the autonomy of the creation. Rather, the divine freedom is the condition of created autonomy. This, however, implies that God's setting free of the creature is a corresponding hiding of himself. Through the act of creation and more so through the act of redemption on the cross, God's freedom acquires the character of latency. God's freedom accompanies the freedom of the creature but in a hidden way.

Before concluding this section, we might say a word about how Balthasar would respond to the Leibnizian position that the world we live in is the best of all possible worlds. At face value Leibniz's (1646–1716) position seems difficult, for there is the obvious fact of overwhelming evil, tragedy and failure, both on the personal and historical level. In response, one must first point to the hidden character of the divine presence in the world. Secondly, one must remember that Balthasar's position is developed in the context of drama. Only in the outcome of the drama can we see whether history has succeeded. Only in the *eschaton* will the cosmos shine in the splendour of the redeemed creation. But in the present the harmony can only be discovered by looking in faith at the cross of Christ.

Still Balthasar does not hesitate to offer us an analogy which can serve to illumine faith. In the world of theatre, it is difficult, if not impossible, to say whether a work of genius could be improved or whether the author given more time could have composed an even greater work. If Shakespeare had lived longer, would his future works have surpassed the sublimity of a *King Lear* or a *Hamlet*? At the same time, if we think of how genius can flow in an almost infinite creativity, we are not surprised to learn that Mozart, without disturbing the unity of his lyrical operas, was able to delete and add arias at will according to the capacities of his singers. What counts in the end is the harmony, unity, balance of parts within the work of art. If God is the divine dramatist, does it really make sense to ask whether he could have done a better job than he has already done? As Balthasar puts it, 'When a composer such as God creates the opera of the world and places in its centre his crucified and risen Son, every fault-finding at his work—i.e. whether or not he could have done it better—must be reduced to silence'.[7]

THE HUMAN RECEPTION OF GOD'S GIFT OF FREEDOM

We have been continually stressing that for Balthasar God's infinite freedom expresses itself in the setting free of the creature. How does this setting free look from the point of view of the human being? In response to this question, Balthasar meditates upon three dimensions of human acceptance of this gift: thanksgiving, prayer, divine indwelling.

We already mentioned above that the human response to God's free self-offering can be nothing other than thanksgiving. The first act of thanksgiving is that which the creature offers to God for his own being. It is not something which human persons offer to God but their own being. Thanksgiving begins in the moment in which I see my own existence as giftedness. In this context Balthasar cites two moving phrases of two outstanding Christian thinkers.[8] The first is that of Nicholas of Cusa who prayed 'How could you give yourself to me if you had not first given me to myself?' The second is a quotation of the philosopher Gabriel Marcel. In his book *The Mystery of Being*, he wrote 'Everything is gift. The receiver of the gift is himself the first gift received.' At the same time, as the quotation of Nicholas of Cusa makes clear, the goal of this first gift is ordered to the second, namely our being assumed into the Christ-form. God's gift of himself is not imprecise, vague, or undetermined. The freedom of faith means determination, destination toward the form of Christ. As St Paul expresses it, 'For those whom he foreknew he also predestined to be conformed to the image of his Son, in order that he might be the first-born among many brethren' (Rom 8:29).

The most concrete expression of the interaction of God and people takes place in prayer, and prayer is the most tangible realization of human freedom. Here Balthasar dares to say that God allows himself to be influenced by our prayers. There is a real dialogue between God and the believer, in which God can take unforeseen initiatives and in which he can respond in unpredictable ways. In Balthasar's opinion, two extremes are to be avoided here. On the one hand, we must not try to reduce God to an unchanging philosophical absolute. This would render prayer impossible. On the other hand, we must avoid a mythological conception of God which reduces him to the level of finitude. In the end, Balthasar argues that the only appropriate approach is Christological. We pray in the name of Jesus with all the liberty of being incorporated into his Sonship. Thus, we have the guarantee that God answers our prayer. Nonetheless, praying in the name of Christ implies praying with his own sentiments, that is, what a heart perfectly open to the Father's will. I must indeed ask, but I must also be prepared to come up against a non-transcendendable limit as Jesus did in Gethsemane.

The final dimension of the human reception of freedom involves two dimensions. First, there is the aspect of God's indwelling me. The mystics describe this as the birth of God in the soul. Just as Jesus took flesh in the womb of the Virgin Mary, so he is born in my heart when I believe. But a true mysticism is never a gift for oneself alone. It is always a gift for the Church. The Lord is born in the Christian so that through faith Christ can be born in others.

Secondly, there is the form of life which the divine indwelling takes. Christ dwells in the believer, to be sure, but he wants his presence to take on a concrete form of life. Here Balthasar appeals to the tradition of Ignatius of Loyola in the *Spiritual Exercises*. If the believer is really free to receive Christ, he is also free to take on the form of life which the Lord enjoins. This choice is always shrouded in mystery. No amount of logical reasoning will reveal it. One must wait in silence for the Lord to speak in his own unpredictable freedom. But one thing is certain. Human openness to God never results in indeterminateness. The gift of freedom always takes shape in a determined form of life in which the believer fulfils the most concrete sending which he has received for the building up of the Body of Christ.

TRINITARIAN FREEDOM: THE PRAYER OF THE ETERNAL PERSONS

In Balthasar's book *Our Mission*,[9] written toward the end of his life, he resolutely affirms that it would be incorrect to try to separate his theology from that of Adrienne von Speyr. One of the areas in which this is particularly true is the field of trinitarian theology. Therefore, in order to complete this picture of the divine freedom, I would like to borrow from von Speyr's book *The World of Prayer*,[10] which consists of talks given by her and edited by Balthasar for publication. Anyone familiar with Balthasar's writings will find echoes of her ideas on trinitarian love scattered throughout the works of her spiritual director.

Let us begin by looking at some of the activities which she proposes as constitutive of the trinitarian life. The first which I would mention is beholding (*Schau*). Each of the persons of the Trinity has his gaze fixed upon the other persons. There is nothing narcissistic about the trinitarian persons. The gaze is away from self toward the other. This beholding is obviously the glance of love. The eye of the lover is fixed on the beloved. Beholding is thus equivalent to love. But, as we know from faith, the mutual beholding of the Father and the Son is at the same time a begetting. Trinitarian love is thoroughly active. The Father and the Son in their mutual beholding breathe the Holy Spirit whose glance is in turn directed back to the Father and the Son from whom he proceeds. In this combination of beholding and begetting we see the origin of that which in the human life of faith forms the unity of action and contemplation.

The believer must learn to act without interrupting the vision.

But von Speyr goes even further and suggests that we can speak of faith as an act of the divine persons. Obviously here we have an idea unknown in the tradition. How can we predicate faith of God? Already we find suggestions toward an answer in Balthasar's writings such as in his essay 'Fides Christi',[11] and in the first volume of *The Glory of the Lord*.[12] For Balthasar, the root idea of faith on the human level is the existential surrender of the human being to God. Faith is not in the first instance an intellectual act. If faith is surrender, then it is not opposed to vision. Rather believing and beholding go hand in hand. When believers entrust themselves to Christ, they actually see what is there to be seen, namely the glory of the Father. But it is equally true that on the human level faith always involves an element of darkness. Von Speyr suggests something analogous in God, which is possible by the fact that God is infinite freedom, and in the Trinity there is infinite space for the free play of love. Without the infinite play-space of God nothing analogous to faith would be possible. But if the three divine persons are infinitely free, then we can speak of a unity-in-tension within the Trinity which makes possible a simultaneous seeking and finding, expectation and fulfilment. As von Speyr puts it, the Son is both the Father's first expectation and the perfect realization of that expectation. The Father thus believes that what he asks of the Son will be and is already fulfilled by the Son. Here von Speyr strains to express the reality of a community of infinite freedom within the limits of finite language.

But if such is the nature of God, then von Speyr can dare to say that we can even speak of prayer within the Trinity. The first dimension of trinitarian prayer is easiest to grasp: namely, adoration. In a certain sense, the nature of adoration flows immediately from the activity we saw above of beholding. In human love the focus is always away from the I toward the Thou. If the love is genuine, I do not look to the other for what he can give me. This would already be egoistic. Nor does love admit of any competition between lovers. One does not love another for something which is lacking in oneself. One loves the other for what one *sees* in the lover, perhaps gifts veiled to the eyes of one who looks with indifference. In valuing others for themselves, I make a place for them in my life. I reverence them for what they are. My love thus creates both nearness and distance, nearness in that I allow the other space, distance in that I do not try to take possession. This phenomenology of human love can be applied analogously to the trinitarian persons. The adoration within the Trinity consists in the reverential beholding and creating of space by one person of the Trinity for the others. The prayer of adoration in the Trinity is the meeting of God with God in love. Each person of the Trinity knows himself as God, but this is not enough. Each wants to know himself through the others. The community of the Trinity includes both the infinite distance and the infinite nearness of adoring love.

Another dimension of prayer which exists in the Trinity is that of petition or request. We already saw above that part of human freedom consists in the liberty to ask in the Son's name with the assurance of being heard. This maturity of requesting and trusting has its roots in the divine life. The Father can ask anything of the Son with the assurance of a response of love. The supreme instance of this is the earthly ministry of Jesus culminating in his passion. Jesus does not suffer an alien fate, for he has already responded to the Father's will to save humankind in an eternal decision of love.

Von Speyr also meditates on the bidding of the Father and the Son in regard to the Spirit. Here too there is requesting but the Spirit does not experience the bidding of the Father and the Son as an alien force. Rather the Spirit so proceeds from them, that in fulfilling their loving will, he is most deeply himself. Here once again we are at the limits of human language and we can only speak in terms of analogies. Von Speyr proposes the following metaphor:[13] it is as if the Spirit, seeing the obedience of the Son, also wants to obey, but the Father and the Son say no to this desire of the Spirit to deny himself. Rather they give the Spirit the freedom to be himself, and hence, as St John says in his gospel, to blow where he wills (John 3:8). And indeed the Spirit does what he wants. However, in love he wants nothing other than what the Father and the Son want. Nonetheless, this is no mechanical carrying out of an alien obedience. Here again the foundation of the Spirit's activity is the infinite freedom of the trinitarian life. The Spirit is infinitely creative in carrying out the requests of the Father and the Son. The paradox of doing the will of another, and at the same time of coming most deeply to oneself, is expressed beautifully by the remarkable saying of St Thérèse of Lisieux, 'The good God always lets me long for what he wants to give me'.

The final act which characterizes the prayer of the Trinity according to von Speyr is decision. Here it is useful to recall what we have already seen in the chapter on theological aesthetics. The divine revelation is never amorphous but always has definite form, and this truth flows from the fact that God himself is not formless but rather, as Balthasar would put it, super-form. Thus von Speyr can say that in God nothing remains undecided. What is it which is decided? We could respond that most fundamentally God decides to be himself, to be the God of trinitarian love and, as Karl Barth would put it, in God's deciding to be himself, he also decides to be our God in advance.

But von Speyr warns us that we must not understand this divine decision in a static way. It is infinitely dynamic and free. Here she plays upon three German words which have the same root, *scheiden* (to divide). In God everything is distinct (*unterschieden*), decided (*entschieden*), and separated (*geschieden*). That is to say, God is the trinitarian mystery in whom the persons are distinct and infinitely separate but equally infinitely one because of the eternal decision of love which is identical with God's being. The divine essence separates itself in the three persons but in the decision of love unites what is separate into unity.

Hence in the divine Trinity there is the infinitely free movement of separation and unification. And since the trinitarian life consists of this divine self-donation, it is no surprise that God acts in the same way in the economy of salvation. Here too we see the continuous movement of separation, decision, unification. The supreme instance of this movement is found in the Eucharist in which Christ distributes himself under the form of bread in the unsurpassable decision of self-donation in order to unite in himself the members of his Body through their participation in the holy communion. Thus, both in God's own life and in his free interaction with the world, every decision is one which both respects the distinction of persons and draws them together into the unity of infinite love.

Notes

1   The Greek Fathers of the Church coined the term *perichōrēsis* to express the circular character of the shared love of the three divine persons. The root of the Greek word is *chōreō*, dance, from which the modern word choreography derives. With this term the Fathers wanted to express the fact that the mutual self-giving of the divine persons can be likened to a circular dance in which every movement of one partner is balanced by the harmonious response of the other partner.

2   An aporia is a philosophical term which indicates a problem without solution.

3   Process philosophy and theology is a movement initiated by two twentieth-century philosophers, Alfred North Whitehead (1864–1947) and Charles Hartshorne (b. 1897) both of whom stressed

the priority of becoming over being and argued that becoming is an element of all being including the being of God.

4   Gerard O'Hanlon in his book *The Immutability of God in the Theology of Hans Urs von Balthasar* (Cambridge University Press, 1990) has shown that Balthasar's language to describe God lies between the metaphorical and the conceptual but in fact is closer to metaphor than to idea. He argues that, although Balthasar's description of God is free of logical inconsistency, it lacks conceptual precision.

5   Nominalism is the doctrine that we can only know the names of things, but not what they really are. Hence it is a doctrine which veers toward agnosticism.

6   Voluntarism maintained that God could do anything he wanted on the basis of his infinite freedom.

7   *Theodramatik* II, 1 (Einsiedeln: Johannes, 1976), pp. 244–5, note 39.

8   For the two qotations following see ibid., pp. 262–3.

9   *Unser Auftrag* (Einsiedeln: Johannes, 1984).

10 Adrienne von Speyr, *Die Welt des Gebetes* (Einsiedeln: Johannes, 1951).

11 See 'Fides Christi' in *Sponsa Verbi: Skizzen zur Theologie* II (Einsiedeln: Johannes, 1961), pp. 45–79.

12 See *The Glory of the Lord* (Edinburgh: T. and T. Clark, 1982), pp. 131ff.

13 See von Speyr, op. cit., p. 53.

8

The paschal mystery

INCARNATION AND CROSS

One of the most striking verses of the psalms is that of Psalm 8 where the psalmist asks in wonder: 'what is man that you think of him, the son of man that you care for him?' The Christian response would be that the mystery of human beings is revealed in Christ. Jesus is the man whom God intended, and we are all called to bear his image. But the tragic fact of our history is that through sin we have failed to reach our God-given destiny. Sin has created an unbridgeable chasm between the human race and God. Since it is impossible for humanity to repair the damage done by sin, and since God is faithful to his covenant love, God comes to our rescue by sending his Son.

The first point which Balthasar makes in reflecting upon the sending of the Son is that his mission consists in both the incarnation and the cross. God not only wanted to assume our flesh; he also wanted to assume the condition of a sinner. In deciding to become a man, Jesus already accepted to bear in himself the hiatus between God and humanity and so to overcome it. Thus Balthasar argues with the Fathers of the Church that the purpose of the incarnation was Jesus' death on the cross. To sustain his position, Balthasar marshals a whole host of patristic witnesses. For our purposes, we can briefly cite two authors. In the Greek tradition, Gregory of Nyssa wrote 'If one examines this mystery, one will prefer to say, not that his death was a consequence of his birth, but that the birth was undertaken so that he could die'.[1] In a similar vein Pope Leo the Great (d. 461) expressed the purpose of the incarnation in these words; 'There was no other motive for the Son of God to be born except to be nailed to the cross'.[2] With this in mind, let us follow Balthasar's reflections as he traces Jesus' journey through the hiatus of sin to the triumph of Easter.

EUCHARIST

As regards the last supper, Balthasar notes that the two elements of the meal and the sacrifice are inextricably linked together. The words over the bread, 'take and eat: this is my body' (Matt 26:26), stress the dimension of the meal, although here too the dimension of sacrifice is not lacking in that the Lucan account adds the words 'given for you' (Luke 22:20). On the other hand, the dimension of the sacrifice is strongly emphasized in the words over the cup where we read 'This is my blood of the covenant, poured out for many for the remission of sins' (Matt 26:28). Obviously here there is a reference to the scene in Exodus 24 where the blood of the animals is poured upon the people and they acknowledge the covenant with the Lord who delivered them from slavery in Egypt.

To grasp the full significance of drinking the blood of Jesus, we must recall that in the Old Testament it was allowed to eat the flesh of animals but not to drink their blood. The blood of the animal offered in sacrifice had to be poured out to the last drop, for the blood, as the symbol of life, belonged to God alone. Also in the Old Testament tradition the blood of a murdered victim cried to God for vengeance. This blood would be remembered by God as evidence against the criminal, and demanded in its turn revenge by shedding the blood of the murderer. Already in the Song of the Suffering Servant we see that it is no longer the blood of an animal which is offered in sacrifice but rather the servant sheds his blood offering himself even unto death and bearing the sins of many (see Isaiah 53:12). The astounding thing about Jesus' offering is that he freely gives himself into the hands of his murderers, and his blood, which belongs to the Father, and which could be recalled by the Father as testimony against the unpardonable sin of the human race, is given back to the murderers so that they might drink of it as a sign that they are indeed reconciled with God. Thus the sign that Jesus' sacrifice has been accepted by the Father consists in the exchange of gifts whereby what has been sacrificed is given back in order to be consumed. In other words, the sacrifice is completed in the communion.

GETHSEMANE

Passing from the upper room to the garden of Gethsemane, we note that here begins the progressive isolation which will reach its culmination in the cry of abandonment on the cross. In Gethsemane Jesus takes the disciples with him but he withdraws to a place apart to pray, as if to say that he alone can enter into the drama which is about to transpire. Three are chosen to remain close to him but they fail to stand the test and fall asleep. Jesus desires that they remain near him and yet the distance between his situation and theirs cannot be overcome.

With this prayer, Jesus enters into the tribulation which characterizes the final clash between God and the power of darkness. This tribulation is signalled by the mood of sadness and anxiety summed up in the words 'Now is my soul sorrowful even unto death' (Matt 26:38). In the Lord's Prayer, Jesus had taught the disciples to pray 'Do not put us to the test but deliver us from the trial'. The trial in question here does not consist in the small temptations of everyday life but in the eschatological struggle between God and Satan. In the garden Jesus enters into this trial, and there is no one to help him. He must face it alone. So horrible is the reality of sin which begins to reveal itself in all its naked vileness that Balthasar describes Jesus' state of soul here as the fear of Gehenna.

In the garden we see the essence of Jesus' filial vocation: the surrender of obedience. All consolation is taken away. Jesus shrinks from the chalice which he must drink. The Father begins to hide himself. There is not the merest hint that Jesus sees all this in the light of the coming Easter. Nor do we find any indication of a titanic, heroic attitude; there is nothing of stoicism. Nor again do the gospels present the picture of the theology of martyrdom in late Judaism. Everything is reduced to the utterly simple: 'Not my will but thine be done' (Mark 14:36). As Balthasar puts it, 'All "meaning" is inexorably reduced to the humble preference for the will of the Father, as loved for its own sake'.[3]

BEING HANDED OVER

Balthasar continually points to the paradox of action and passion in the paschal mystery. The tension is vividly expressed in the Greek word *paradidonai*, to hand over. On the one hand, Jesus is the protagonist in this drama. He freely lays down his life, and St Paul does not hesitate to say that he hands himself over for our sakes (Gal 2:20). But at the same time the active disposal of himself means that Jesus lets himself be disposed of. As Jesus himself expressed it at the moment of his arrest in the garden of Gethsemane, 'It is enough. The hour has come; the Son of Man is handed over into the hands of sinners' (Mark 14:41). The handing over of which Jesus speaks finds its concrete realization through the actions of those such as Judas, Pilate and the Jewish people who cry for his death. But Balthasar argues that the ultimate handing over has its origins in the trinitarian decision of the Father to send the Son to save the human race from the abyss of sin. Paul expresses this conviction most radically when he says 'God did not spare his only-begotten Son but handed him over for our sakes' (Rom 8:32). Although Jesus says 'yes' to this being handed over, we must not rob this *para-didonai* of its horrifying effect. The scriptures express this dimension with words such as the 'power of darkness' (Luke 22:53) and 'night' (John 13:30). Jesus is delivered into the yawning chasm of sin in which the blackness of loneliness prevails. In this night all vision is taken away. As Balthasar would put it, the only thing which is left to Jesus is relentless and blind obedience.

THE CROSS AS JUDGEMENT

In the Old Testament there are many words which render the idea of justice. But whereas to our contemporary ears the idea of God's justice evokes sentiments of fear, for a Jew God's justice implied his saving mercy. Thus the psalmist could confidently pray 'In you, O Lord, I take refuge, I will never be disappointed; for the sake of your justice save me' (Ps 31:1). Or again, 'Judge me according to your justice, O Lord my God, and let them not rejoice over me' (Ps 35:24). Because God is just, he has a special concern for the poor, the widow, the orphan, the oppressed. God's justice is thus equivalent to his saving deeds. To express this aspect of God's justice the Hebrews employed the word *sedek*.

Another word for justice is God's *mispat*. This word can be used to express the verdict rendered in a trial, In the juridical process there is the accuser, the accused and the judge who renders *mispat*. The same word is also used to express God's justice with regard to the covenant. He must see that the conditions of the covenant are fulfilled.

It is clear in this perspective that God's justice is gracious and saving. But this graciousness does not exclude God's anger. For the sake of the covenant God must manifest his wrath toward his people when they break the covenant bond. But he manifests his justice in this way for the sake of his mercy, to bring his people to repentance.

Jesus' life is the proclamation of God's saving mercy to sinners. He remains faithful to this mission even when he is rejected by his people. His death as the extreme manifestation of God's loving mercy is the supreme revelation of God's *sedek*. But it is also the manifestation of God's *mispat*. God remains faithful to the broken covenant. Insofar as Jesus identifies with sinners, the wrath of God for sin falls upon him. Moreover, in the legal terminology of the court, Jesus is accused. He is accused by the Romans of being a revolutionary. He is accused by the Jews of being a blasphemer.

But in the trial scene Jesus does not seek to defend himself. He remains silent. On the one hand, he does not accuse his accusers. On the other hand, he absorbs the wrath of God, so that all hatred and lovelessness is swallowed up in his self-surrender to God and to us. Thus sin is annihilated, literally swallowed up in love. God's justice has triumphed over human infidelity and has created anew the covenant, and since Jesus does not accuse us, we are spared the judgement of condemnation which we deserve and instead receive the divine pardon.

In Pauline terms this is the doctrine of justification. Christ has objectively obliterated the reality of sin. And by being incorporated into him, we are inserted into his justice which is the saving mercy of God. By being transferred to his place, we are made right. The same truth is expressed in Johannine language when Jesus declares 'Now is the judgement of the world' (John 12:31). Christ's death represents the turning point of history. On the cross sin is blotted out and eternal life is made available for men and women. And if the cross is the crisis of the world in objective terms, this crisis becomes real for each man or woman when confronted with the decision of faith. Those who believe are not condemned. They find their place in Christ and pass from the darkness to the light. On the other hand, the failure to believe is already condemnation, for in this case one is left to oneself in the abyss between God and the sinner which only Christ was able to cross (see John 3:17–21).

CRUCIFIED WITH CHRIST

We have repeatedly returned to the theme of the hiatus between heaven and hell. As we shall see shortly in our exposition of Holy Saturday, part of the mystery of Christ's passion is that he goes down into this abyss from which only the Father can save him. In any case, it is clear that since Jesus alone is the Son, no one else can throw open the gates of hell. This mission is reserved for the Son alone and only his cross brings redemption.

As he begins his journey toward hell, he states explicitly 'Where I am going, you cannot come' (John 13:33). And yet part of the mystery of the Christian life is that by the fact of justification and the outpouring of grace into our hearts, we are indeed invited to share in his cross. What was a sheer impossibility before the resurrection becomes part of the grace of Easter existence. Obviously there is no question of usurping the uniqueness of Christ's death. But part of the fruit of that death is that we are inserted into his reality. Indeed, as Paul would say, the mystery of our baptism is that we have died with Christ (Rom 6:8). But if this is an objective fact, it is equally true that Christ invites us in some way known to him alone to share in his passion. In some way we will be called to conform our lives to his cross. His cross shapes our form of life. Paul verified this truth in his own life as an apostle where the sufferings of his apostolate configured him to his crucified Lord so that he could say 'I have been crucified with Christ' (Gal 2:19).

Moreover, this mystery of our co-crucifixion with Christ is not just a matter of personal piety. For just as the Lord's death bore within it an infinite fruitfulness, so the share which Christ gives us of his passion is meant to bear fruit for others. This is the sense of Paul's words in Colossians 1:24, 'Now I rejoice in my sufferings for your sake, and in my flesh I complete what is lacking in Christ's afflictions for the sake of his body, that is, the church'. The mystery of Christian discipleship is that Christ invites us to participate in what is uniquely his, and at the same time promises us that our share in his sufferings will not be in vain, but in a manner perhaps unknown to us will serve for the building up of his body and the coming of his kingdom.

THE THEOLOGY OF HOLY SATURDAY

Continuing with the stages of Christ's entrance into the paschal mystery, we pass from the events of Good Friday to the silence of Holy Saturday. One of the immediate contrasts we note is that if Good

Friday represents Jesus' active self-surrender, Holy Saturday symbolizes his identification with us even to the depths of the absolute helplessness of the sinner. Jesus is no longer able to do anything. He can merely be with us in the solidarity of the powerlessness of the sinner.

We have often spoken of the yawning gap between the living God and the dead sinner. Balthasar frequently refers to this gap as a hiatus. We make a mistake if we think of the passage from Good Friday to Easter as a simple succession of events. Between Good Friday and Easter Sunday there is the incommensurability of the hiatus. Insofar as Jesus radically identifies with us sinners, he is not able to leap over the hiatus. Nor can we conceive of Easter as a circumventing of the hiatus. Rather Jesus goes down into the hiatus itself in such a way that the hiatus becomes part of the victory. Our salvation does not consist in escape from death nor in life on the other side of death. Rather the victory passes through death. Jesus' being translated into the hiatus is the mystery of Holy Saturday.

To understand the full implications of these New Testament affirmations, we must probe the Old Testament background of Holy Saturday. One aspect of this mystery is found in the Israelite conception of the realm of the dead which the Hebrews called Sheol. The most important point is that Sheol is the exact opposite of everything the Hebrews understood by God. God is the God of the living, full of vitality, the Creator God. Those who stand in his presence praise him. Where there is God, there is life. By contrast, Sheol is the pit, a land of darkness where there is no genuine life, for there the dead are cut off from the source of life. It is the land of silence where there is no communication with the world of the living and where the dead are no longer able to sing the praises of the Lord. It is a shadowy existence, for these spirits are mere dust. The psalmist, therefore, places his confidence in God that the Lord will save him from going down into the tomb and into the pit. He confidently makes his imploration citing as his motive that if the Lord will save his life, he will continue to praise him. Typical is the supplication of Psalm 6: 'Turn, O Lord, save my life; deliver me for the sake of thy steadfast love; for in death there is no remembrance of thee, in Sheol who can give thee praise?' (vv. 5–6).

A second theme also enters here as background and is perhaps even more important than the first, namely the motif of God's abandonment of his people. We have already spoken of God's covenant love which is faithful and which has the right to expect a response of fidelity from his people. We have also touched on the theme of God's wrath. When God's love is rejected, the only response appropriate to God's holiness is that of anger. One of the constant images of God's relation to his people in the Old Testament is that of his abandonment of Israel. To get some idea of the terror which God's wrath inspired in Israel, Balthasar suggests that we look at such passages as Leviticus 26:14–39 or Deuteronomy 28:15–68 where God pours out his threat of judgement upon his people because of the covenant which has been broken. Israel's terror before her enemies is nothing in comparison with the dread which she experiences before a vengeful God. On the one hand, God threatens Israel with his absence. No longer will Israel stand under the divine protection. The divine presence even withdraws from the temple because of Israel's idolatry (see Ezek 10:18f.; 11:22f.), but worse yet, God makes himself to be the enemy of his people (see Lam 2:5). If the destructive power of the neighbouring pagan states is great, how much more terrifying is the destructive power of Israel's God. In short, the most frightening possibility of all for Israel is to be utterly rejected by the God of the covenant. As Lamentations expresses it, 'Have you rejected us completely, is your wrath without measure?' (Lam 5:22). One of the symbols of this wrath without measure was developed in the intertestamental period, namely, the valley of Gehenna set aflame to consume the reprobate. Jesus often makes allusion to this fire of Gehenna, for example, when he warns that it is better to cut off a hand or foot which is a source of temptation and to enter into life maimed than to be cast into Gehenna with two hands and feet and perish in an unquenchable fire (see Mark 9:43ff.).

Balthasar's theology of Holy Saturday hinges on the fact that Jesus with his death enters into the experience both of the lifeless passivity of Sheol and of the utter rejection of Israel prefigured already in the Old Testament in such figures as Job and the servant of Yahweh. With the experience of Holy Saturday Jesus goes down into the 'underworld'. How are we to interpret this fact? First, Balthasar notes that there are two *loci classici* for Jesus' descent into the underworld. In 1 Peter 3:19 the author states that after his death Christ went and preached to the spirits in prison. Later in chapter 4 the same theme is touched upon, where it is said that the gospel was preached even to the dead (v. 6). Obviously Balthasar recognizes that we are dealing with certain patterns of Hebrew thinking which today we would call mythological. Nonetheless, he argues that these ideas contain a profound theological truth.

In Balthasar's reflections upon this text of Scripture, he brings into relief two important dimensions. First, he observes that the whole context for the allusion is Christian baptism. Probably the whole of the first letter of Peter is an Easter baptismal homily. The author of 1 Peter is comparing the waters of the flood with the waters of baptism. Both were waters of judgement. But whereas the waters of the flood served to destroy the unfaithful people of God (the author notes that only eight people were saved in the ark: 3:20), the waters of baptism are oriented to salvation and indeed to the salvation of the entire people of God. Secondly, Balthasar points out that important background for these chapters of 1 Peter is the apocryphal work Ethiopian Enoch, written in 37 BC, where in chapters 12–16 there is a midrash[4] upon the story of the fallen angels in Genesis 6. According to the midrash, Enoch is sent into Hades to the angels who beg the pardon of God. But his mission is not one of consolation or of mercy, for the Lord God commands him to communicate to the angels that they will have no peace at all. By contrast, Jesus is sent among the dead with the mission to proclaim their release from prison.

The principal difference between Balthasar's interpretation of Jesus' descent among the dead and the more classical approach is that for Balthasar Jesus' descent is no triumphal journey into the underworld. Nor in his opinion do we have to see Jesus as engaged in some activity such as preaching the gospel. Without a doubt the underlying motive of Balthasar's interpretation are the experiences of the mystics, especially those of Adrienne von Speyr, who have described the torments of abandonment in hell. In line with this approach, Balthasar interprets the preaching of the gospel in the underworld as the making known by the presence of the dead Christ of the objective fact of redemption. According to Balthasar, all the activity involved in Jesus' redeeming work is limited to the active self-surrender on the cross on Good Friday. Holy Saturday rather expresses the passive solidarity of Christ with the dead. On Holy Saturday the fruits of Christ's active struggle on Good Friday are made manifest in the underworld.

Let us then unfold in greater detail the theological significance of Christ's solidarity with the God-forsaken in Sheol. The basic affirmation of Balthasar is that Jesus' descent among the dead means that he experienced the full reality of hell. In turn, this thesis contains at least two explanatory affirmations. First, Jesus entered into the radical passivity and helplessness of the sinner. He was reduced to the utter lifelessness of the corpse. In the striking phrase of Balthasar, he became a cadaver-obedience. Secondly, he felt the full weight of abandonment and rejection by the Father. Because Jesus freely bore our sins, on the cross he was confronted with the reality of sin in all its naked horror. Sin is hatred, separation from God. On the cross, Jesus knew what it means to be utterly rejected by God.

In this Balthasar says that Jesus experienced the reality of hell. In fact, he says that hell is a Christological concept which takes its definition from the experience of the cross. Theologically speaking, hell means total darkness, absolute despair, complete forsakenness. In the Old Testament we do not find such an experience. Even in the bitterest moments of Israel's darkness, when it seems that God has forsaken her and abandoned his covenant, there is always the promise of the coming redeemer. The light of the coming Christ makes its presence felt even in the shadows of Sheol. But on the cross the light is extinguished. As St John puts it, 'Men loved darkness rather than the light, for their deeds were evil' (John 3:19). Thus, Balthasar stresses the spiritual dimension of Christ's experience of hell. It is the separation from the Father that constitutes hell for the Son and this suffering cannot be measured either in weight or in time. The hell of Jesus' God-forsakenness is timeless.

A HELL FOR CHRISTIANS?

The fundamental Christian affirmation of faith is that Christ has suffered hell in our place. Since he has put himself in the place of our sin, we no longer need fear rejection by the Father. The fact of our sin destined us for the isolation of a loveless hell, but the fact of our union with Christ destines us always to companionship, whether in life or in death. What then are we to make of the constant affirmation of both Scripture and tradition that hell is a real possibility even today for the man or woman who is unfaithful to Christ and his commandments?

If we look at the New Testament, we see that a problem which the early Christian communities had to face was that of apostasy. What is the fate of those who have known Christ and accepted him, only later to turn away? Of such persons the letter to the Hebrews says that they on their own account crucify the Son of God and hold him up to contempt. Their fate can only be that of a fertile land which after having been irrigated with the fruitful rain of heaven produces thorns and thistles. The end of such a barren land can only be to be burned up (see Heb 6:4–8). In other words, for those who are unfaithful to Christ the New Testament develops the concept of the second death which consists in a new fire of Gehenna. This is the Christian hell.

In regard to this second hell, Balthasar says that we can and must make a number of affirmations which, however, cannot be reduced to a neat system. First, we must say that God has destined all men and women to be saved. As Karl Barth so clearly recognized, there is only one destination of the human race, and that is to salvation in Jesus Christ. Hence without a doubt God's saving will is universal. But, secondly, we must admit that man and woman remain free. Hence there is always the possibility that someone will hold out to the end and reject Christ's grace.

What Balthasar strongly rejects is the conviction that someone is in hell. The New Testament clearly affirms that hell is a possibility, but never declares that anyone is in hell. This conviction, which was taken for granted over the centuries, Balthasar traces back to St Augustine. He rejects this idea for a number of reasons. First, he says that this conviction undermines the saving efficacy of Christ's death. Theologians as distinguished as Newman argued that part of Christ's suffering on the cross consisted in the sense of the futility of the passion. But Balthasar asks: how do we know this, who are we to set limits to the efficacy of Christ's saving death?

Secondly, there is the relation between love and hope. The question of hell is in its roots a question of hope. As Balthasar puts it, dare we hope that all men and women are saved? He would argue that unless we can hope for all, then we cannot be in solidarity with all. In other words, the scope of our love would already be restricted. For this position Balthasar appeals to a number of thinkers such as Gabriel Marcel and Vladimir Soloviev (1853–1900). Marcel, for example, wrote 'For there can be no particularism of hope; hope loses all sense and all force if it does not imply the statement of an "all of us" or an "all together"'.[5] Elsewhere Balthasar cites the statements of Jürgen Verweyen, 'Whoever reckons with the possibility of even only *one* person's being eternally lost *besides himself* is unable to love unreservedly'.[6]

The phrase 'besides himself' points to the true significance of the scriptural and dogmatic affirmations about hell. They are in their core warnings. Only in this way can they be considered part of the Good News. They are not statements of fact but appeals to our liberty and summons to conversion. As Cardinal Ratzinger observes, the purpose of the dogma of hell is 'to bring man to grips with his life in view of the *real possibility* of eternal ruin and to understand revelation as a demand of the utmost seriousness. The fundamental reference to this *redemptive meaning of the dogma* must therefore serve as both a boundary marker and an internal guideline for all speculation in this area.'[7]

Finally, as we already indicated above, Balthasar warns us that when we talk about the dogma of the Christian hell, we are dealing with diverse affirmations that cannot be reduced to a neat system. And the ultimate reason for this is that here we are confronted with the unfathomable mystery of God who is both infinitely just and infinitely merciful. However difficult it is for us to grapple with the divine attributes, we know that they cannot be played off, one against the other. On this point Balthasar points out how Thomas Aquinas seeks a solution in the approach of St Anselm who wrote 'If you punish the evildoers, you are just because this befits their misdeeds; but if you spare the evildoers you are likewise just because that corresponds to your goodness' (*Proslogion*, 10). Reflecting upon this text, Aquinas comments 'But between the misdeeds of the creature and the goodness of God there is no equilibrium, which means that justice with respect to the former is subordinated to divine mercy, indeed must be virtually a mode of this mercy' (*Summa* I, q. 27). Balthasar would argue that even today we cannot do better than to echo the sentiments of Aquinas which perceive God's justice as a form of his mercy and therefore lead us to *hope* that all will be saved.[8]

THE ABYSS TRANSCENDED: EASTER SUNDAY

It is interesting to note that Balthasar calls the section dealing with the resurrection in his lengthy work *Mysterium Paschale* 'The Journey toward the Father'. With this title he wants to indicate that the resurrection means not only that Jesus is alive but that he has returned to the glory of the Father. As we saw in treating Christology, Jesus' descent was for the sake of his ascent. During his lifetime, he did not seek his own glory. His one concern was always to do the will of the Father. This obedience carried him to the depths of his descent into hell where he took upon himself the sins of the world. Now in giving back his human life, the Father restores him to the glory he had before the foundation of the world. Hence the resurrection is the Father's response to the Son's obedience.

THE NATURE OF THE RESURRECTION-EVENT

Perhaps the most radical problem which confronts the theologian in talking about this event is to clarify what is meant by resurrection. Here Balthasar follows the tradition of Karl Barth who saw the resurrection as an event without analogy. Never has such an event happened before and never will it happen again, for this event signifies God's definitive victory in human history over the forces of sin and death. This event represents the turning point of human history. It is the hinge on which all human history hangs. On the one hand, it is an event within history in that as far as it touches us we can date it at a particular point within the history of the world. On the other hand, since resurrection means that Jesus breaks the vicious circle of sin and death and returns to the Father, it is an event without parallel, an event which transcends history. Balthasar calls it a metahistorical event.

If this is the case, we immediately have the problem of the accessibility of this event to scientific investigation. As regards this problem, Balthasar makes a number of points. First, he notes that the Scriptures emphasize the objectivity of the event. We can see the accent upon objectivity in such kerygmatic formulae as Luke 24:34, 'The Lord has truly risen and appeared to Simon', or Acts 2:32, 'God has raised Jesus from the dead'. At the same time, granted the reality of the event, Balthasar nonetheless affirms that we have access to this event only in faith. The risen Jesus is there to be seen but he can only be perceived in faith. This affirmation is totally consistent with what we have already seen in the theological aesthetics, namely that faith and vision are not contradictories but rather grow in a direct proportion.

What then are we to say of the resurrection from the point of view of the empirical science of history? Here Balthasar follows the position of Heinrich Schlier[9] in arguing that we are dealing with a limit-situation. Since the resurrection is metahistorical, scientific history as such cannot grasp it. But at the same time Balthasar asks if we are bound to accept the account of reality proposed by historical positivism according to which the only real events are those encompassed by space and time. To this question Balthasar resolutely answers in the negative. He notes moreover that the question cannot be settled by science alone, for underlying the scientific method are presuppositions about reality which faith cannot accept. Does this mean that the resurrection is not an historical event?

In response to this question Balthasar makes use of the distinction in German between the *historisch* and the *geschichtlich*. The *historisch* is that which is open to scientific investigation. In this sense the resurrection is not historical in that we cannot find evidence for it which is historically secure (*historisch gesicherte*) but the resurrection is historical in that it touches upon and illuminates our human historicity (*Geschichtlichkeit*). In Balthasar's words, there is evidence for the resurrection in this sense, that is, evidence 'which impinges itself in an historically convincing manner'.[10] In other words, the resurrection confronts us with the question of the meaning of history and of our historicity. Science as such cannot decide this question. Hence we cannot come to the texts of Scripture without presuppositions. If we are convinced that death and finitude are the last words about human existence, then we will never be open to what the texts want to say. Rather, according to Balthasar, we should follow the advice of Schlier and let the texts say what of themselves they want to say.[11] And the texts want to say that the resurrection is an event which impinges on our human history in such a way as to bring it to fulfilment. Or, as Jürgen Moltmann would put it, resurrection is a history-making event.[12]

PRE-COMPREHENSION OF THE RESURRECTION-EVENT

Although the resurrection is an event without analogy and although the category of the eschatologically new can never be grasped within the limits of the old, Balthasar does admit that there was a preparation for the new in the Old Covenant. As always, the preparation does not have an intelligibility in itself but is revealed as preparation from the perspective of the fulfilment. In this context Balthasar indicates the points which prepared the way for the event of the resurrection and its acceptance in faith by the disciples.

First, there was the ever-growing consciousness in Israel that its God was the Creator God, the God of the living and not the God of the dead. This faith was reinforced especially during the period of the exile. Here Israel was reduced to the point of obliteration. If the desert was the time of trial, the exile was the reduction to nothingness. Had the God of the covenant abandoned Israel or was her God impotent? In the return from exile Israel learned that her God can create out of nothing.

Secondly, in the centuries immediately preceding the coming of Christ, there was the growing conviction of a general resurrection of the dead. Especially in the light of persecution and the fate of the martyrs, Israel was led to see that God would vindicate those who died for their faith. At the same time there was absolutely no hope for a resurrection of one man before the general resurrection. In this sense Jesus' resurrection came as the totally unexpected action of God. Still, in light of the apocalyptic background, it is clear why the church linked together the resurrection and the second coming of Christ.

Finally, there is the aspect of the ministry of Jesus himself which is intrinsically linked to his person. As we saw in the section on Christology, Jesus made a claim for himself which required a vindication. Either the Kingdom would come as he announced or he would be proved a fraud. In this context, his death represented the shattering of the hopes of the disciples who placed their faith in him and in his mission. But in spite of the despair provoked by his death, the claim of Jesus prepared the disciples to understand the meaning of the resurrection when it happened.

ENCOUNTERS WITH THE RISEN CHRIST

If we ask about the epistemological foundations of the event of the resurrection, we are obviously led to speak of the appearances of the risen Christ to the disciples. The first point which Balthasar notes is that it is best to understand these appearances not as visions but as encounters with the risen Jesus. Important here is the biblical phrase *ōphthē* ('he was seen'), which suggests the Old Testament experience of the theophanies of God to his people. Clearly, no human person as such has the capacity to see God. God can only be known or seen where he makes himself visible. The bridge between people and God cannot be created from the human side but must be erected by God. In the resurrection appearances all the initiative lies with Jesus. He appears unexpectedly. Suddenly Jesus is in their midst. Moreover, these experiences are intensely personal. Heart speaks to heart. One thinks of the moment of revelation in the garden when the eyes of Mary Magdalene were opened to recognize the risen Jesus when he called her by name (John 20:16), or the experience of the disciples on the road to Emmaus when their hearts burned within them as they conversed with the risen Christ (Luke 24:32).

Secondly, Balthasar notes that these encounters involve the dimension of conversion. One recalls that during his lifetime Jesus was able to read the hearts of men and women (Simon the Pharisee, the woman with the flow of blood who touched his garment, Judas who would betray him, and so on). His meetings with such people brought them to a recognition of their true state. It was often a confessional situation. So too after the resurrection. When the disciples meet Jesus, his gaze penetrates their hearts, his look cuts them to the quick. Thus, for example, Thomas is led to recognize his unbelief (John 20:28). The eyes of Paul are opened on the Damascus road to see that he is the worst of sinners in that in persecuting the Church of Christ he was persecuting Jesus himself (Acts 9:4–5). Peter's triple denial of the Lord is forgiven by his three-fold confession of love before the risen Christ (John 21:15–19).

Thirdly, Balthasar notes that these encounters lead to a recognition of Jesus' true identity. What was hidden during his lifetime now becomes fully revealed. Here for the first time we find the explicit confession of his divinity: 'My Lord and my God' (John 20:28) and the acknowledgement that Jesus is worthy of divine worship. As we read in Matthew's gospel, when the disciples recognized who he was, 'They took hold of his feet and worshipped him' (Matt 28:9). As risen Lord, Jesus is worthy of the same adoration and glory as the God of the Old Testament. For as risen, the Father has glorified him to share the same honour and dignity as himself.

Fourthly, with the experience of the resurrection, the disciples are given an understanding of what previously was closed to their eyes. On the one hand, Jesus opens their eyes to understand the meaning of the Old Testament and how it is fulfilled in him. As Luke 24:27 expresses it, 'Beginning with Moses and all the prophets, he interpreted to them in all the scriptures the things concerning himself'. On the other hand, they are given a comprehension of all that happened during the lifetime of Jesus which they failed to understand at the time, especially as to the nature of Jesus's identity and the meaning of his paschal mystery.

The last aspect which Balthasar emphasizes in the encounters with the risen Jesus is the dimension of mission. These encounters never leave the disciples closed in upon themselves. There is no question of their wallowing in a sentimental clinging to the person of Christ. Rather he sends them out as witnesses. They are given the mission to proclaim the word that he is risen and thus to found the church upon this word. The Word which became dumb on the cross must now be proclaimed through these witnesses. 'Go therefore and make disciples of all nations, baptizing them in the name of the Father and of the Son and of the Holy Spirit, teaching them to observe all that I have commanded you' (Matt 28:19–20). The shattered and fearful disbanded group of disciples is transfigured into an audacious college of apostles.

THEOLOGICAL DIMENSIONS OF THE RESURRECTION

Among the many theological aspects of the resurrection which Balthasar touches upon we can here take note of three. First, the resurrection of Jesus in the flesh is the fulfilment of the incarnation of the Logos in the flesh. God has fully pledged himself to this world, and this so radically that he has become bodily in it. Sometimes exegetes point to what they call a 'materialization' of the resurrection in the Easter accounts, for example, in the fact that Jesus eats the fish (Luke 24:43). But Balthasar holds that the true danger lies on the other side, namely in an excessive spiritualization. Rather God wants us to find our salvation in the body, and the supreme proof of this is the eucharist.

A second dimension which Balthasar discusses is that of the time of the resurrection. In his view Christian faith in the resurrection opens up a new understanding of time. On the one hand, the apocalyptic view of the late Old Testament has been overcome in that the world is no longer waiting for the one who is to come. If Jesus' contemporaries looked for the appearance of the Son of Man, the New Testament writers were convinced that Jesus is the expected Son of Man. Thus he who is to come is the one who has already come. On the other hand, the Platonic world-view has been definitively overcome with the resurrection of Jesus. True fulfilment does not consist in an eternal realm beyond time. Rather as the Risen One, Jesus makes himself present to every time. The eternal impinges on every moment since Jesus is alive and makes himself felt. As Balthasar puts it, 'The Risen One can only work and rule as the present one, because he is the past and the coming one: "the same yesterday, today and forever" (Heb 13:8)'.[13]

Finally, Balthasar brings out the trinitarian dimension of this event. As we have already noted, the principal agent in the resurrection is the Father. In the descent among the dead, Jesus has fully identified with the powerlessness of the sinner. He must await the Father's action. God the Father, the Creator God, on Easter Sunday restores to Jesus his human life and brings Jesus to the glory he had before the foundation of the world. The New Testament is unanimous in attributing this action to the Father. Typical is St Paul: 'Christ was raised from the dead by the glory of the Father' (Rom 6:4).

But a closer look at the gospels equally reveals that as Son Jesus already contains the power of the resurrection in himself. The clearest witness to this fact is St John who records Jesus' ringing affirmation, 'I am the resurrection and the life' (John 11:25). Do we have here a contradiction? Can Jesus have the fullness of eternal life and yet have to wait the action of the Father to raise him? Balthasar argues that there is no contradiction, for Jesus as Son is precisely receptivity, obedience toward the Father. Everything he has he receives. As Balthasar expresses it, 'If it belongs to the supreme obedience of the Son that he lets himself be raised by the Father, it belongs no less to the completion of his obedience that he lets it be "granted" him by the Father to "have life in himself"' (John 5:26)'.[14]

Finally, the event of the resurrection is an event of the Holy Spirit and this in two senses. First, the Holy Spirit is the instrument through which the resurrection takes place. Thus, for example, Paul can argue 'If the Spirit of him who raised Jesus from the dead dwells in you . . . he who raised Christ Jesus from the dead will give life to your mortal bodies also through the Spirit which dwells in you' (Rom 8:11). Secondly, the Holy Spirit is the medium in which the resurrection takes place. Again Paul brings out this point in the kerygmatic formula 'He was manifested in the flesh, vindicated in the Spirit' (1 Tim 3:16).

The Spirit dimension of the resurrection is extremely important, for it points to the goal of God's saving relations with the world and indeed to the purpose of the incarnation. We have already seen in Christology that Jesus is the man whom God intended. He is the new Adam. But as Paul stresses, it is precisely the mission of the new Adam to become a life-giving Spirit (cf. 1 Cor 15:45). Hence with the resurrection God's purposes for the world are fulfilled, in that the fullness of the Spirit which was in Jesus now becomes available for all men and women. Sharing in that Spirit we too become the new creation that God intended from all eternity. Jesus' exaltation to the Father is in no way his being withdrawn from us. Rather he comes back to us with an infinitely greater intimacy, indwelling us through the Spirit, thus enabling us to participate on this earth in the eternal love of the Trinity itself.

THE THEOLOGY OF THE FORTY DAYS

Since we are dealing with the full sweep of the paschal mystery in this chapter, it would be fitting to conclude our reflections with a word on the forty days of our Lord's tangible presence with his disciples after

Easter culminating in the ascension. We have already seen that for Balthasar the resurrection is the overcoming both of the apocalyptic and the Platonic view of time. The accent in Christian theology lies on the present time of the risen Christ. This is the fullness of time in which the eternal makes itself felt in the temporal. For Balthasar, the tangible proof of the eternal in the temporal is the presence of the risen Christ with his disciples after his resurrection. In these forty days we see that time and eternity are not contradictories. Between Christ's time and our time there is an encounter, indeed there is an influence and counter-influence. One sees this in the story of the disciples on the road to Emmaus where Jesus makes himself present and where the disciples constrain him to remain with them. These encounters become a paradigm for all future encounters with the risen Lord in the Church.

We already saw in the chapter on divine and human freedom that the marvel of Christian faith consists in the fact that God allows himself to be influenced by our freedom in the life of prayer. He really hears and really responds. All this is foreshadowed in Christ's dealings with the disciples during the forty days. As I say, the forty days become a paradigm for our understanding of the relation between God's time and our time. During the life of Jesus, eternity and time intersected but in a hidden way. Now with the forty days the veil is drawn aside. God's eternity becomes visible in the encounters with the risen one. God makes himself visible to show us that from now on the time is fulfilled. From now until the end of time it will always be possible to encounter him.

The ascension marks the end of this visibility. Jesus returns to the Father but his presence is not taken away. Rather he is still available, but once again his revelation takes place in hiddenness. We must seek his face in faith, as he is truly present under the veil of the sacramental signs or under the cover of our suffering brothers and sisters. But in either case the truth remains the same. Christ is truly present with us. The long-awaited future is here, for Jesus is the *eschaton*, he is the fullness of time, and because of his presence in the midst of us every moment of time becomes a *kairos* in which God can be found.

Notes

1   Gregory of Nyssa, *Oratio Catechetica* 32 (PG 45, 80A) as cited by Balthasar, *Mysterium Paschale* (Edinburgh: T. and T. Clark, 1990) pp. 20–1.

2   Leo the Great, *Sermo* 48, 1 (PL 54, 298) as cited by Balthasar, ibid., p. 21.

3   Balthasar, ibid., p. 106.

4   A midrash is an exegesis or an interpretation of the Old Testament by a later writer. Often within the Bible there is a midrash of a text of the scripture by a later biblical author.

5   Gabriel Marcel, 'Structure de l'Espérance', cited by Balthasar, *Dare We Hope That All Men Be Saved?* (San Francisco: Ignatius Press, 1988), p. 81.

6   Jürgen Verweyen, *Christologische Brennpunkte*, cited by Balthasar, ibid., p. 211.

7   Balthasar, ibid., pp. 198–9.

8   For this discussion, see Balthasar, ibid., pp. 154ff.

9   Heinrich Schlier is a contemporary Catholic biblical scholar.

10 See Balthasar, *Mysterium Paschale*, p. 228.

11 Ibid., p. 190.

12 Moltmann develops this thesis at length in *Theology of Hope* (London: SCM Press, 1967).

13 *Herrlichkeit* III, 2, 2 (Einsiedeln: Johannes, 1969), p. 340.

14 *Mysterium Paschale*, p. 207.

9

Theology of redemption

INTRODUCTION

A central motif in Balthasar's theology of redemption is that of
covenant. God wishes to enter into a covenant of friendship with
humanity. The idea of the covenant of friendship is closely linked to
another central theme in Balthasar, the bridal union between heaven
and earth which is the goal of all God's saving activity. And so God
takes the initiative with Israel for the sake of a covenant with all
humanity, and God is faithful to his initiative because he is faithful
to himself (2 Tim 2:13). The difficulty, however, is that the more
God places himself in self-gift to his people, the more humanity
refuses his offer. Israel is an adulterous people who goes in search of
other gods. As we read in Hosea 11:2, 'The more I called them, the
more they went from me; they kept sacrificing to the Baals and burning incense to idols'.

Here then is the dilemma which God himself must face and which
stands at the centre of every attempt to understand the redemption:
how can God be faithful to himself and his covenant when his
human partner is unfaithful? On the one hand, there is the question
of God's mercy. God's compassion leads him to seek to rescue a
people who has fallen into the wretchedness of sin, a people who has
forfeited life for death. On the other hand, God's justice must come
into play. The order of the covenant must be restored. But how
restore the covenant, if humankind for its part is not in a position to
re-establish it? Thus, from one point of view, it would be unworthy
of God not to redeem us. But, from another perspective, it would be

unworthy of God to redeem us by trampling upon our freedom. The divine creativity must seek a way to redeem us which involves our freedom.

CENTRAL THEMES OF THE REDEMPTION

Throughout the history of Christianity, theologians have sought to elaborate the meaning of the solution which God the Father has found in Christ to resolve this dilemma involving his justice and mercy. As we shall see, the history of theology is replete with systems which try to capture the significance of the redemption. But Balthasar argues that any system as such will fail to do justice to the reality of the redemption, which shatters our human categories of thought. Nevertheless, every theological attempt at synthesis must take as its basis a number of New Testament affirmations, which in themselves do not provide a conceptual system, but which illumine aspects of the mystery which must be preserved in a dialectical tension.

In *Theodramatik* III[1] Balthasar lists five indispensable New Testament affirmations which form the foundation of any Christian theology of redemption. First, there is the reality of the double surrender of the Father and the Son. The Father does not spare his only-begotten Son (Rom 8:32) and in turn the Son is willing to lay down his life for our sakes (Gal 2:20; John 10:17). Second, there is the idea of the *admirabile commercium*, the exchange of places between the Son and the sinner. Jesus, the Son, takes our place, is made sin in our place (2 Cor 5:21) in order that we might assume his place and become sons in the Son. A third theme is that of the liberation of humankind. This liberation is expressed in the New Testament with the help of different images: as freedom from the law (Rom 7:4); as deliverance from the power of darkness (Col 1:13); as liberation from the devil (John 8:44) and from the elemental spirits of the universe (Col 2:20); as ransom from slavery (Mark 10:45). But if, on the one hand, redemption means freedom from, more significantly it means freedom for. In the positive sense redemption is our incorporation into the divine life. And finally, the basis of the entire drama of redemption is nothing other than the divine love. All the action has its source in the Father who so loved the world that he gave his only-begotten Son not to condemn the world, but that the world might be saved through him (John 3:16-17).

Looking at these five elements of redemption, Balthasar observes that the shortcomings in the history of theology derive from the fact that in a given system one element is exaggerated at the expense of other dimensions. The task of a theology of redemption is to seek to balance these different aspects of redemption, and the theologian must realize that they can never be reduced to a monolithic system. Finally, Balthasar notes that although it is important to seek new language in which to express these New Testament affirmations, we must beware lest the new language water down or dissolve the truth which the New Testament proclaims. One such case of a new language which fails to do complete justice to the New Testament witness, is, in Balthasar's opinion, the replacement of the language of substitution with that of solidarity.

HISTORY OF THE DOCTRINE OF THE REDEMPTION

Balthasar develops his theology of the redemption in dialogue and confrontation with the major figures of the Christian tradition. The first period which he takes into consideration is that of the Fathers where the principal emphasis lies in the doctrine of the *admirabile commercium* (wonderful exchange). Typical of the approach of the Fathers is Irenaeus (*c.* 130–*c.* 200): 'The Word of God became what we are in order to perfect us to become what he is'.[2] Another witness cited by Balthasar is the Cappadocian Father, Gregory Nazianzen (*c.* 329–*c.* 389), who affirmed that Christ played our role in the drama of salvation in our name. According to Gregory, 'Christ bears me entirely with all that belongs to me'.[3] In Balthasar's opinion, this identification of Christ with the sinner is certainly the heart of the redemption, but here he raises a critical question in regard to the Fathers. Have they really taken the doctrine of Christ's identification with us to its depths? How radical is Christ's identification with humankind? Is Christ really made one with sin or does he only take upon himself the consequences of sin? At times the Fathers elicit a doubt in regard to the radicality of Christ's identification, for example, when St Augustine (354–430) interprets the Pauline doctrine that God made him who knew no sin to be sin in the sense that Jesus becomes only an offering for sin. Typical is the following saying of Augustine: 'Christ found us lying in guilt and punishment, he assumed the punishment and took away the guilt and the punishment'.[4]

Turning to the Middle Ages, Balthasar devotes a considerable amount of attention to St Anselm (*c.* 1033–1109). Today Anselm's theology hardly meets with appreciation. It is often considered too juridical. God seems preoccupied with his own honour. Moreover, Anselm, in seeking the necessary reasons for the incarnation and the redemption, seems to fall into a type of theological rationalism. To these charges Balthasar offers a number of responses.

As regards rationalism, the necessity of which Anselm speaks is not the necessity of fate. It can only be a necessity which is compatible with the freedom of God and of his covenant partner. To use a technical expression of Anselm, the necessity in question is that of a *necessitas sequens*, that is, the necessity that follows God's free decision to create humankind and destine it for a share in his life. What *must* God do if this plan is not to founder?

Secondly, Balthasar notes that in no way are we talking here of Christ's buying back our salvation from an angry God. Christ is not in any way constrained to change the mind of the Father. In fact, everything proceeds from the Father's will to save, from the divine mercy. Balthasar brings as evidence a text of Anselm where he asks 'What could be more merciful than when the Father says to the sinner who has no means to redeem himself?: take my only-begotten Son and offer him for you, and when the Son says: take me and redeem yourself'.[5]

Finally, Balthasar suggests that the key for interpreting Anselm positively today lies in the theology of covenant. At the heart of the covenant lies the idea of the freedom of the partners. God's covenant with humanity is first of all an act of his sheer unbounded grace, but Balthasar notes that the covenant also includes a dimension of justice. God has a right to the fidelity of his covenant partner just as Israel has a right that God remain faithful to his promise. But if humanity breaks the covenant, God is placed before a dilemma: how remain faithful to himself as God of grace without surrendering the aspect of justice which the mutual swearing of the covenant partners entails?

For all Balthasar's appreciation of St Anselm, he realizes, however, that a number of elements are not adequately developed by the mediaeval doctor. Too short space is given to the motif we saw in the Fathers, namely the exchange of places between God and the sinner. Not enough attention is given to the dimension of the eternal trinitarian obedience of the Son which grounds the drama of redemption. Very significantly for Balthasar, even less attention is given in Anselm than in the Fathers to the fact that Jesus really does become sin for us. For Anselm sin as such does not touch Jesus at all. Finally, there would be need to develop in greater profundity the organic connection between Christ and the rest of humanity. Jesus does not die just as an individual but as representative of the human race and as Head of the Mystical Body.

One of the most important dialogue partners for Balthasar is Luther. Although Balthasar can be severe in his criticism, he remains fascinated by Luther, for in some ways Luther comes closest to his own project of developing a dramatic soteriology. For Luther, as for Balthasar, the cross must stand in the centre of every attempt to understand God's dealings with humanity. Luther more than any other theologian gives adequate weight to the exchange of places between Christ and the sinner. God becomes what we are, sin, so that we might become what he is, righteousness. God descends into hell so that we can ascend into heaven.

The difficulty is that Luther's approach to the Christ-event is permeated by serious contradictions. The first contradiction is found in the area of Christology and the doctrine of God. Here we encounter Luther's famous doctrine of *Deus sub contrario* (God under his contrary). Typical is Luther's remark: 'God cannot be God, he must first become the devil, and we cannot come into heaven, we must first descend into hell'.[6] What does Luther mean by this? First, that Jesus experiences God-forsakenness. Jesus on the cross lives the experience of the wrath of God. All the wrath that God would pour out upon the sinner he pours out upon Jesus. Hence Jesus becomes the first human being to embody the doctrine of *simul justus et peccator*.[7] Perhaps one could even go further and call Jesus *simul justus et damnatus* (justified and damned at the same time). In Luther's view, Jesus upon the cross bears the extreme contradiction of holiness and sin, and he is able to bear the contradiction because of the identity of his divine person, even though Balthasar would argue that Luther so stresses the separation in the act of abandonment on the cross that the Reformer falls almost into a type of Nestorian dualism.[8]

But the most urgent question which Balthasar addresses to Luther is whether we can in fact talk about a contradiction either in Jesus or in God. In Balthasar's opinion, Luther's theology is marred by a fundamental inconsistency in the doctrine of God. Luther is haunted by two faces of God, the wrathful and the merciful. For Balthasar, on the contrary, God is pure unbounded love. The Son's willingness in obedience to identify with humanity even to the God-forsakenness of the cross is not an alien obedience but the filial obedience of the Son's desire to co-operate with trinitarian love.

Moreover, on the cross, there is no contradiction in Jesus. On the cross Jesus bears the negativity of sin but without inner division. He sustains the contradiction of sin in an attitude of perfect surrender to the Father and to us. The cross signifies not contradiction but love in the midst of contradiction.

The other neuralgic point in Luther's theology follows from the first and regards his Christian anthropology. Does Luther end up as well in a dualism in regard to the man or woman justified by God's grace? Here Balthasar finds that Luther does not have a consistent position as regards justification and sanctification. In fact, Balthasar argues that Luther drives a wedge between them. On the one hand, sinners are justified by grace alone. They can do nothing to merit this justification; they must receive it as a sheer unmerited grace. On the other hand, Luther does not fail to exhort the sinner to prayer, penance and works of charity. This second aspect of the Christian life falls under what Luther calls *donum* (gift). Justification is sheer grace but the *donum* must be cultivated. Luther takes the *donum* seriously, and yet if he is not going to fall back into the works righteousness which all his theology has sought to avoid, the *donum* must be continually referred back to the *gratia* (grace).

But has Luther developed here a position free of contradiction? It would seem not. On the one hand, all is grace; on the other hand, the grace must be cultivated with human effort. Luther does not shy away from stating the contradiction in explicit terms: 'The sin remains and does not remain; it is taken away and not taken away'.[9] Nowhere does the contradiction become more apparent than in the temptations against faith. What are people to do when they are shaken by tormenting doubts or when they are terrified by their sins? Luther's answer would be: believe all the more, take refuge in Christ. But is not this very advice an encouragement to the very type of works righteousness which Luther's doctrine of grace is meant to overcome?

In summary, Luther's anthropology, just as his Christology, rests upon a dualism. He has shattered the ancient vision of unity defended by the Fathers and has driven a wedge between human justification and sanctification. Although his soteriology is dramatic, he has not been able to do justice to the central affirmation of faith that God is love and to the consequence which follows from it, namely that men and women, liberated from sin in Christ, are in fact healed so that love becomes a genuine human possibility.

Turning to contemporary theologians, we can look briefly at two thinkers to whom Balthasar devotes considerable attention, namely Karl Rahner and René Girard.[10] As is well known, Rahner's method is transcendental.[11] He begins with the human search for God. The human person is constituted as an openness to the Absolute Mystery whom we call God. Jesus Christ is understood as the fulfilment of this human orientation toward the Mystery. Although Rahner adopts a starting point from below, he admits that this openness from below can only be fulfilled by a corresponding movement from above. The incarnation of Jesus Christ is the point where the movement from above and that from below meet.

As regards the death of Jesus, Rahner believes that the Anselmian approach offers difficulties for the man or woman of today. It seems to me that Rahner is willing to accept the idea of Christ's death as satisfaction for sin, but he warns us that such an idea must be interpreted properly. For example, we cannot say that Jesus changes the mind of God. Such an affirmation would already go against the notion of God's immutability. In what sense, then, does the death of Jesus accomplish something? Here Rahner is reluctant to employ the category of efficient causality. In his opinion, Jesus accomplishes our salvation by being the victorious sign of God's grace in human history. But in order to be this sign of grace, Jesus must in his whole life surrender himself to the Father. This surrender must also embrace his death, for death is that reality which lets the whole of life appear as a totality. What is important, then, is that Jesus is faithful to his mission right up to the end. He does not hold back his fidelity even in the crisis of his death. Thus his death as culmination of his whole life has saving efficacy.

Balthasar's criticisms of Rahner are trenchant.[12] He rejects the transcendental method as reducing Christ to the level of human expectations. For Balthasar, the Christ-event is so new that no human categories can capture it. It is completely unpredictable. Secondly, Balthasar believes that the dramatic dimension is completely lacking in Rahner's anthropology. The incarnation and the cross seem to add nothing to the grace already given to humanity with the creation. For Balthasar, on the contrary, the cross is the event which turns around the whole course of human history. Balthasar finds this dimension lacking in Rahner. Moreover, he does not believe that Rahner takes into account the fact that Christ bore the sin of the world on the cross. For Balthasar, the death of Christ was different from every other human death in that Christ bore the full weight of sin in our place. According to Balthasar, Rahner's theology of the death of Jesus reduces Christ's death to a mere example to be imitated. In his view, Rahner has undermined the unique efficacy of the cross as an event which reverses the whole tide of the drama between God and humankind.

The final major author whom Balthasar examines is René Girard, especially in his work *La violence et le sacré*.[13] In Balthasar's opinion this work is of great significance, for it is the clearest example of a dramatic soteriology on offer today. Girard is highly influenced by Freud, especially by his work *Totem and Tabu*. He locates the source of the sacred and indeed of all culture in the mechanism of the scapegoat. At the source of the human personality is the phenomenon of the desire. And desire for Girard is linked to imitation. When I see what another has, there emerges in me a desire to possess. This desire in turn provokes in me thoughts of violence. I am willing to kill to possess that which I desire. A primitive example of this is the murder of Abel by his brother Cain. But the violence in turn produces in me a terrifying guilt. And so the individual seeks a scapegoat on whom he can unload his guilt. Here there enters the phenomenon of sacrifice. One or more persons choose a victim on whom they load their guilt. In killing the victim, they experience a cleansing and a catharsis.[14] Human history can be viewed as a series of acts of violence followed by the search for a scapegoat and catharsis. The phenomenon of peace is always temporary and will be followed by new acts of aggression as well as the search for new scapegoats. According to Girard, testimony for this interpretation can also be found in literature. One thinks of Oedipus Rex.[15] His eyes are gouged out. He must be punished for his sin, but in bearing this act of violence he becomes a source of blessing for the people of Thebes. Violence and benediction go hand in hand.

The phenomenon of the scapegoat is also at the heart of the biblical faith. In the Old Testament God is seen partly as a violent God who demands bloody sacrifice from his people. A powerful example is that of the suffering servant. According to Isaiah, God has placed upon him all our crimes (Is 53:6). At the same time the servant does not respond with violence but willingly bears the sins of his people. He does not open his mouth to lament but lets himself be led to the slaughter. The complete overcoming of the scapegoat mechanism takes place in the event of Jesus' cross. Jesus exposes the mechanism for what it is. His death is a sacrifice in the sense of self-offering, but it is not the placating of a God desiring violence. In this sense the death of Jesus represents the overcoming of the concept of sacrifice.

We can note that Girard's interpretation of the sacred is largely

Barthian in its orientation. In other words, Girard makes a sharp contrast between religion and faith. He interprets religion as the sacred which has its roots in the mechanism of the scapegoat. For this mechanism to work it must remain hidden. The coming of Christ represents the exposing of the mechanism. By exposing it Christ overcomes it for he robs it of its power. Hence the death of Jesus means the end of religion and the sacred. He has revealed God to be the God of non-violence. God does not desire a bloody victim to appease his violent needs. With the cross of Christ sacrifice is at an end.

Although Balthasar finds Girard's vision powerful, he finds it equally wanting. First of all, Balthasar argues that Girard's interpretation of the redemption is too narrowly psychological. Humankind needs more than psychological cleansing. He asks whether Girard has an adequate concept of sin. Secondly, in line with Girard's Barthian heritage, Balthasar believes that this vision takes too little into account the role of the freedom of God's covenant partner. Apart from Christ people have absolutely no freedom. They are totally corrupt. The mechanism of the scapegoat annuls every aspect of human freedom. But if this is so, is any drama between God and people really possible? Finally, Balthasar criticizes Girard's understanding of the sacrifice of Christ. Must we not say that in some sense the Father desires the sacrifice of Christ? If Christ overcomes the need for sacrifice, does this do away with the sacrificial dimension of the eucharist?

Girard has undoubtedly seen something of critical importance for soteriology, namely that the God of the Bible is no violent God. In the cross we see that God allows that humankind heaps its violence upon him without his reacting with violence. By taking the violence into himself, he turns it into love. But in the end Girard leaves us with an unanswered question. Not only must we seek to understand the attitude of men and women toward Jesus, but we must also comprehend the Father's attitude toward Jesus. If the Father is sheer unbounded mercy, and if he is thus from all eternity willing to forgive sinful humanity, then why does the Father will the cross? Balthasar says that we must seek an answer to this question by probing anew the meaning of God's justice. To be sure, God is no violent God, but he is a God of justice. The central question of the doctrine of redemption thus becomes: what is the relation between God's love and his justice which leads the Father to ask the Son to die on the cross to redeem the world from its sin?

BALTHASAR'S SOTERIOLOGY

Having looked at Balthasar's treatment of the various approaches to the theology of redemption in the history of theology, we can now turn to his positive contribution to soteriology. The first point to note is that Balthasar grounds the whole drama of redemption in the inner divine life. Here he wants to avoid two pitfalls: first, the temptation to identify God and the suffering of the world as do Hegel and some of his disciples such as Moltmann. Secondly, there would be the opposite danger of exaggerating God's immutability in a way which would remove him from participating in the tragic human situation.

Balthasar's approach is to view the divine life itself as the primordial drama in which the action of the cross is situated. God's life is not static but dramatic, and the drama consists of the eternal self-emptying of the three persons. The Father does not want to be the Father apart from the Son, and so from all eternity he gives his being away to the Son. At the same time, the Son is eternal response to the Father. He surrenders his being back to the Father in love. So radical is his *kenosis*[16] toward the Father that the Son is willing to undertake the mission toward humanity, and as Karl Barth would put it, travel into the far country. Finally, the Holy Spirit does not want to be God for himself, but in the depths of his being is totally referred to the Father and the Son. Speaking figuratively, Balthasar affirms that the Trinity is the mystery of infinite nearness and infinite distance. There is, so to say, infinite space between the persons, for each of the persons makes room for the others. But at the same time the distance is bridged over by love. Since the Trinity is in its being divine *kenosis*, we can understand how the drama of salvation is kenotic. The self-emptying of the eternal Trinity makes possible the self-emptying of the divine persons in the history of salvation. Balthasar sees the unfolding of this story of salvation as progressive levels of self-emptying: from creation, to incarnation, and finally to cross. If the cross is the supreme moment of 'God-lessness' (*Gottlösigkeit*), this event has its roots in the God-lessness of the trinitarian life, that is, in the fact that none of the persons retains the divinity for himself but gives it away.

A second major theme in Balthasar's soteriology is that of representation, the fact that Jesus takes our place and becomes sin for us. Here we must confront the question which emerged from the discussion with René Girard. Who lays the sin upon Jesus? In a certain sense, the first response would be that we human beings do. We have seen how the history of salvation consists in a continual series of the divine self-offer of love. But the more God offers, the more human beings reject his love. Certainly, this law can be verified in Jesus. He is God's final offer to his people. He comes at the last hour with a final offer of mercy and amnesty for sin. Yet humanity once again says 'no'. The Son is rejected and crucified. But in a second sense, the answer to our question must be Jesus himself. At first, it would seem that Jesus is the victim in the story of the passion. But a closer reading of the story indicates that Jesus is the true protagonist. As he puts it in St John's gospel, 'No one takes my life from me but I lay it down of my own accord. I have the power to lay it down and to take it up again' (John 10:17–18). So Jesus willingly enters into the passion and takes upon himself the sin of the world.

But the most difficult part of our reflection is the relation of the Father to Jesus in the mission to bear the sin of humankind. Does the Father lay upon Jesus human sin? If so, does this make the Father a sadist? Is such a conception unworthy of the name God? Here Balthasar says that we must distinguish between divine punishment and divine wrath and we must clarify the relation between God's wrath and mercy.[17] Although some theologians have taught that the Father punishes the Son on the cross, Balthasar never teaches this doctrine. What he does say is that the whole biblical tradition affirms the wrath of God, and, indeed, that Jesus on the cross experiences this wrath. How should we understand this concept of the wrath of God?

God's wrath is linked to his holiness. Moreover, God's wrath cannot be separated from his love. Since God is love, he must reject sin. Sin, which is hatred, cannot be incorporated into the divine life. Hence when God encounters lovelessness, he can only react with wrath. But, as Balthasar insists, God pours out his wrath on the sinner for the sake of his mercy. God manifests his wrath so that the sinner will be converted and so will be saved.

On the cross, Jesus so identifies with sinners that the Father sees in him the 'no' of humanity. To that 'no' the Father can only react with wrath. Hence Jesus dies in the experience of the total abandonment of God. But at the same time Jesus dies in absolute obedience to the Father. He remains the pure 'yes' of obedience. Thus the Father also sees in him a radical 'yes'. As we have seen before, the death of Jesus is pure love in the midst of contradiction. He is separated from the Father insofar as he is made sin. He is in union with the Father insofar as his death represents his loving obedience.

Moreover, the fact that Jesus lets the sin of humanity be heaped upon himself, coupled with the fact that he accepts the Father's wrath without breaking his surrender of love, means that all the negativity of sin is swallowed up in this act. The poison of sin has been consumed and exists no more. Here is the catharsis of which Girard speaks. Sin has been engulfed in love. The 'yes' of Jesus to the Father and the 'yes' of the Father to Jesus and in him to all humanity has been victorious in the midst of the 'no'. Thus, what seemed God-forsakenness turns out to be trinitarian love. What seemed the victory of sin and death turns out to be the victory of love and the welling up of new life in the resurrection. As the biblical scholar Vincent Taylor observes, never has there been a more radical dichotomy between appearance and reality. As he puts it, what is experienced is the opposite of what in fact happens.[18] In conclusion, the drama of the passion is the drama between the Father and the Son but also the drama between God and man insofar as Jesus is truly one of us. Hence this drama is no mere play-acting. Two freedoms are involved, divine and human. God has found a way to save us in which all the initiative is his and yet which nonetheless maximizes human freedom to its fullest potentiality.

The next major theme of Balthasar's soteriology is our reception of the trinitarian life through the death and resurrection of Jesus. His death has not just the negative result of taking away sin. Positively, from the paschal mystery flows the gift of the Holy Spirit. If human created freedom as such means the capacity to receive a gift and to be able to return that gift to the Father in thanksgiving, with the gift of the Holy Spirit that gift receives a new depth. Those who are in Christ participate in his Sonship. They can offer not only themselves to the Father; they can offer the Son as well. This is the mystery of the eucharist.

In this context we could say a word about Balthasar's understanding of the human being as *imago Dei* (image of God). Here he takes up the doctrine first hinted at in Genesis and developed at length by the Fathers that the human being is made in the image and likeness of God. According to Genesis 1:26 God says 'Let us make man according to our image, according to our likeness'. The notion of image and likeness is expressed in the Hebrew by the two words *salam* and *demut*. What is the meaning of these two words? As regards *salam* (image) Balthasar notes that exegetes are agreed on at least two points. First, the word implies the bodiliness of the creature. Secondly, the word implies that what distinguishes humans from the other animals is that they have a relationship with God. Thus, Balthasar argues that, although the term analogy as such is not used, we are justified and even required to see in this verse the foundation of the doctrine of the analogy of being, that is, the creature in its very being is meant to correspond to the reality of God.

Secondly, although Balthasar admits that the distinction between image and likeness did not play a significant role in Old Testament exegesis, it is nonetheless legitimate to interpret this text in the light of Christ, in other words, to read the text in the light of the Church's faith. He notes that the Fathers saw two points of significance in the distinction. First, in the idea of image they saw the ontological aspect of the creature, the relationship to God which could never be lost, for it belongs to the constitution of the person. In 'likeness', they saw the ethical dimension, the possibility of losing the filial relationship with God through sin. In fact, the history of sin demonstrates precisely that this second aspect was lost with the fall of Adam. The second aspect of significance which the Fathers highlight is eschatological, in other words, the distinction between the first and the second Adam. Humans were created in relationship to God, but the first Adam exists for the second. Creatures exist in God's plan so that they can be gifted with sonship in Christ. Christ is the new Adam and in fact only of him can we say 'He is the image of the invisible God' (Col 1:15). But we have been created to receive his likeness. This point is expressed beautifully by St Paul when he writes 'For those whom he foreknew he also predestined to be conformed to the image of his Son, in order that he might be the first-born among many brethren' (Rom 8:29). This conformity to his Sonship is the fruit of the passion. When in baptism we receive the gift of the Holy Spirit we are re-created according to his likeness.

A further dimension of soteriology is our incorporation into the church. We are not saved only for ourselves. By the gift of the Holy Spirit one not only receives the new life of the Trinity; one is also incorporated into the Body of Christ. One becomes a branch of the vine and so is able to bear fruit. Here we are confronted with a fundamental mystery of Christianity. Christ's death is absolutely unique. No one is able to do what he alone did. For only he as the Son could bear the sin of the world. When we look at the life of Jesus, we see that although the disciples followed him, they could not accompany him into his death. As Jesus puts it, 'Where I am going, you cannot follow' (John 13:36). And yet, after his death, the disciples must follow him even in this. So fruitful is his passion that its grace flows into us and enables us to share in his fecundity. Since we are in him, we can truly offer the eucharist with him. Thus, on the one hand, his death is exclusive, but at the same time through the mystery of Christ we are included in it, so that our lives must be bearers of grace for the others. As our Lord says explicitly, 'I have chosen you that you should go and bear fruit, fruit that shall last' (John 15:16).

The last point which we can mention in regard to Balthasar's theology of redemption is that he sees the death of Jesus as the key which unlocks the enigma of the mystery of human death. For Balthasar, human death, looked at from the perspective of philosophy alone, remains a riddle without solution. He argues that death involves at least three important dimensions. The deepest, in his opinion, is the fact that each man or woman experiences death as threat, fate, doom. Every life is carried forward under Damocles's sword of death. At the same time, in the history of culture, death is often linked to guilt. Very often death is seen as something deserved, Here is a theme often found in tragedy where one must suffer for one's hubris by the punishment of death. Perhaps the clearest instance of death as retribution is the case of criminals who pay for their crime with their lives. But even under this aspect there is no ultimate resolution to the enigma of death. In an execution criminals pay their debt to the state, but does this resolve the problem of their guilt before the living God?

A second way of looking at death is that of an interpretation of life. Death is the event which sums up and gives meaning to one's life. But this dimension is more often than not undermined by the first. The threads of fate are often cut before the pattern is completed. How often is a life's work or flowering human relationships destroyed by an untimely death!

The final aspect is that of death as deed. Here perhaps one tries to anticipate death by taking one's fate in one's hands. Perhaps in giving one's life for others, the others are spared. But even here, for these others, the moment of fate is only postponed. Balthasar asks if in anticipating fate one has really overcome it or merely resigned oneself to it. In Matthew Arnold's (1822–88) dramatic poem *Empedocles on Aetna*, the philosopher throws himself into the crater to grasp at divinity. But is this nothing more than the wish-fulfilment of phantasmagoria?

The only way to overcome death is to find a weapon which is deadlier than death and which strikes the lethal blow at the dimension of doom in death. For Balthasar, the weapon with which Christ removes the sting of death is his obedience. In a certain sense, Jesus from the beginning lives under the sentence of death. The Son has become incarnate in order to die for us. Moreover, Jesus sees clearly that his mission moves him inexorably toward Jerusalem and the clash with the religious authorities, a conflict which will lead to his crucifixion. But he lives all this not as doom or fate but as obedience freely given. Everything in his life is ordered to his hour, but at the same time this hour is not grasped in a titanic way. Rather Jesus receives it from the Father's hand. Since he has overcome the sting of death (fate), his death succeeds in perfectly interpreting his life. His death offered as sacrifice to the Father for our sakes reveals that his whole life has been a self-giving of love. And finally we see that his death becomes the deed *par excellence*. As we saw in the chapter on the incarnation, Jesus is the Word of the Father, but on the cross the Word becomes the deed of love. 'Greater love has no man than this, that he lay down his life for his friends' (John 15:13).

In conclusion, the death of Jesus represents the culmination of the drama of divine and human freedom. The history of God's 'yes' to humankind has provoked the growing crescendo of the human 'no'. On the cross Jesus takes this 'no' upon himself and turns it into a 'yes'. The 'no' of sin led to the insurmountable wall of death. The 'yes' of Jesus breaks down the wall and leads men and women into the new life of love of the Trinity. The Spirit, poured out upon humankind from the cross, opens up the new possibility of human existence lived out in a daily act of eucharist.

Notes

1 *Theodramatik* III (Einsiedeln: Johannes, 1980).

2 Irenaeus, *Adversus Haereses* V, prol. as cited by Balthasar, op. cit., p. 225.

3 Gregory Nazianzen, *Oration* 30 as cited by Balthasar, op. cit., p. 230.

4 Augustine, *S. Guel.* 31, 3, Morin 558 as cited by Balthasar, op. cit., pp. 231–2.

5 Anselm, *Cur Deus Homo* l. II, c. 20 as cited by Balthasar, op. cit., p. 236.

6 Luther, *Commentary on Psalm 117*, as cited by Balthasar, op. cit., p. 268.

7 According to this doctrine of Luther, the Christian remains justified and a sinner at the same time. He remains a sinner but God looks away from his sin and casts his eyes on Christ's redeeming grace alone.

8 Nestorianism is a heresy attributed to Nestorius (d. *c.* 451), Bishop of Constantinople, according to which in Christ there are two persons. Such a position destroys the unity of Christ.

9 Weimar edition of Luther's works, 56, 270 as cited by Balthasar, *Theologik* II (Einsiedeln; Johannes, 1985), p. 309.

10 René Girard is a contemporary Protestant theologian, heavily influenced by Karl Barth, who has sought to enter into dialogue with the psychoanalytic tradition of Freud.

11 The transcendental method looks for the conditions of possibility for a given experience, in this case, for the Christian faith.

12 See 'Exkurs. Zur Soteriologie Karl Rahners' in *Theodramatik* III, pp. 253–62.

13 René Girard, *La violence et le sacré* (Grasset, Paris, 1972) as cited by Balthasar, *Theodramatik* III.

14 The term catharsis has its origins in Greek tragedy and signifies the purification of an emotion through the participation in the drama. Girard's theory of the scapegoat mechanism indicates the purification of aggression through the sacrifice of the scapegoat.

15 The story of King Oedipus was frequently recounted in Greek literature, e.g. in the drama *Oedipus Rex* by Sophocles. Oedipus unwittingly kill his own father and marries his mother, for which he inflicts on himself the penalty of being blinded. But his suffering in turn brings blessing upon his people.

16 The word *kenosis* comes from the Greek language and means 'self-emptying'. The concept of *kenosis* has been important in theology, especially in connection with the interpretation of the Christological hymn in Paul's letter to the Philippians (2:5–11).

17 In the reflection which follows we see a further clarification of the point made in Chapter 8 on the paschal mystery where I discussed Balthasar's ideas on the cross as God's judgement.

18 Balthasar appeals to Vincent Taylor's commentary upon St Mark's gospel. See *Theodramatik* III, p. 312.

10

Church and eucharist

INTRODUCTION

One of Balthasar's richest essays bears the title 'Who is the Church?'[1] The title already gives us an important clue about how Balthasar thinks of the Church. The Church is not a *what*. Hence Balthasar rejects any impersonal approach to the Church. He is for this reason wary of the image of the Church as the people of God. Although in a certain sense this is a true image, Balthasar fears that such an image is too linked to an Old Testament understanding of covenant, and is also in danger of reducing the Church to a sociological reality. At the same time he wants to avoid a clericalization of the Church. Balthasar grew up learning a scholastic theology according to which the form of the Church consists of the hierarchy, and the matter of the Church is the laity, who are to be governed by the clergy.[2] Such a view, however, is inadequate to the personal dimension of the Church. The structures of the Church exist to serve persons and every person in the Church becomes a person through the unique mission received by Christ. Who then is the Church? In what sense is the Church a person? If the Church is a person, how are the persons who are believers incorporated into the Church?

THE CHURCH AS THE BODY OF CHRIST

As usual, Balthasar's mode of thinking is guided by images. The first key image that invites theological reflection is that of the Body

115

of Christ. Obviously here we are dealing with a biblical motif. In the first place, one associates this image with Pauline theology. Paul asks 'Do you not know that your bodies are members of Christ?' (1 Cor 6:15). Later he explains: 'Just as the body is one and has many members, and all the members of the body, though many, are one body, so it is with Christ' (1 Cor 12:12). Here we have to do with an organic model: Christ and the Christian form one, undivided reality. Although the organic unity of the Church is perhaps best expressed by the Pauline image in the Bible, other biblical images point to the same truth, for example, the organic unity that exists when the branch is united to the vine (see John 15). So deep is the unity of vine and branches that one life pulses through both.

In Balthasar's theology of the Body of Christ, a number of points deserve to be underscored. First, in this theology, the source of the being and the unity of the Church lies in Christ. Christ lets the Church be by creating members and inserting them into his reality. Thus, the Church is not a reality separate from Christ, rather the Church is Christ's prolongation in space and time. Balthasar calls the Church in this sense the *Elongatur Christi*.[3] In this context, it is clear that the Church is primordially personal, for the Church is nothing less than Christ himself. Just as King Louis XIV so identified himself with his country to declare that he was France in person, so Christ can say 'L'église, c'est moi' (I am the Church). Here Balthasar develops the Augustinian theology of the *totus Christus* (the whole Christ). Who is the Church? The Church is Christ, but the total Christ, head and members. As St Augustine would put it, when speaking of the Church, 'We are Christ' (*Christus sumus*).

Another point of emphasis in this vision is the link between incarnation and Church through the mediating concept of bodiliness. We have seen in other chapters how important for Balthasar is the fact that God enters into our flesh. We have seen that for Balthasar only Christianity takes the reality of the world with full seriousness. Balthasar is suspicious of any spirituality which prompts a flight from the world. In Christianity, to be sure, there is the gift of the Spirit, and it is the pneumatic Christ who dwells in our midst. But for Balthasar wherever there is the Spirit, there is a dynamism by which the Spirit seeks to become bodily. Hence the risen Christ becomes bodily in the flesh and blood of the Church. There is no access to him which can bypass this stumbling block. And the clearest manifestation of the bodiliness of the risen Christ and of the bodiliness of the Church is found in the eucharist. 'Unless you eat the flesh of the Son of Man and drink his blood, you have no life in you' (John 6:53).

THE CHURCH AS BRIDE AND MOTHER

If the first image stresses the organic unity of Christ and the Church, the second image of bride and mother stresses their real distinction. We, human believers and members of the Church, are not Christ. We are sinful creatures who stand over against him in obedience and love.

In this second image the archetype of faith and hence the archetype of the Church is Mary, the mother of the Lord. Balthasar stresses that during the first millennium of the Church's existence Mariology focused on the role of the maternity of Mary. A parallel was drawn between the physical birth of our Lord from the virgin and the birth of Christians from the womb of the Church. Theology linked together the scene at Nazareth with that of the cross where Jesus gave his mother to be the mother of all believers.

The first point which we can notice here is that the Fathers show how the real source of Mary's maternity was her faith. They are not so interested in her physically giving birth to Christ. What interests them is the faith which makes possible God's act of incarnation. For the Fathers, there was always an intrinsic link between *caro ex qua* (the flesh from which) and *fides ex qua* (the faith from which). Hence Mary becomes mother by her 'yes', a 'yes' which is first uttered in the annunciation and which will carry her as far as the cross. Standing beneath the cross, uttering her final silent 'yes', she becomes the mother of all believers. She is thus the mother of the Church, the archetype of all who respond to Christ in faith. What she did, the Church must do. As she bore Christ in her womb, so all Christians must let Christ be born in their hearts.

No doubt it is more difficult to understand the image which developed in the second millennium, namely that of Mary as bride. The mother is also the spouse. To understand this image, we must first of all note its roots in the theology of the fourth gospel. In John's account of the passion, Jesus hands over his mother to the beloved disciple. As we saw above, symbolically this action shows that Mary becomes the mother of believers. But in John's gospel, at the moment of the death of Jesus, his side is opened with a lance so that blood and water flow out. Jesus gives all that he has, even the last drop of blood and water, for us. But in this self-giving there is manifested an infinite spiritual fecundity. From his open side the Church is born. This symbolic action can only be fully grasped if it is linked to the story of the creation of Eve in the book of Genesis. Since God does not wish Adam to be alone, he places Adam in a deep sleep, and from the rib of Adam's side he creates Eve to be his partner. Similarly in the death of Jesus, the new woman is created from the side of Christ. On the one hand, this new woman is Mary who by her 'yes' prepares the way for the new creation. On the other hand, the new woman is the Church, created by the grace of Christ, to be the bride without spot or wrinkle (see Eph 5:27).

To appreciate these ideas more fully, we must link them to how Balthasar understands the reality of sexuality and its relation to sin. For Balthasar, in the condition of paradise, man and woman would have lived in a state of primordial unity which would have combined virginity and fecundity. Balthasar admits that we cannot imagine how this could be, but he does affirm that procreation would not have taken place under the conditions of sexuality as we now know it. Balthasar believes that after the fall it is extremely difficult to express sexual relations in a way which does not have a degree of egoism. Moreover, in our present human condition, sexuality is intrinsically bound up with the reality of death. The propagation of the human race is a way of overcoming the necessity of having to die. In this context, Balthasar argues that Jesus could never have been born from a sexual union of the type we know. His birth must already be a sign that his life means the breaking out of the vicious circle of sin and death.

Here Balthasar draws together into a unity the three doctrines of the virginal conception of Christ, the immaculate conception of Mary, and the birth of the Church. The definitive victory over sin and death took place in the self-giving of the cross. In that event, as we saw above, Christ gave birth to the Church as the *ecclesia immaculata*. But this event had to be prepared. And so, from all eternity and in view of the saving efficacy of the cross, Christ chose Mary and prepared her to offer her 'yes' to the Father's saving plan. The Church can be born from the side of Christ if Christ is born from the Virgin Mary. But this birth presupposes that Mary is prepared by the grace of Christ to offer her 'yes' to the Father. Thus, the *ecclesia immaculata* is bound to *Maria immaculata*.

And so Christ in his death creates the Church as his bride. The Church as spouse stands over against him as a subsistent reality. The Church is Christ's partner who must say 'yes' to the obedience of love as Mary did. Who then is the Church? Balthasar answers that in one sense the Church is Mary. In her the essence of the Church is fully realized. She is the Church as Christ intended. Thus, in the catholic understanding of ecclesiology, the Church is not merely an ideal to be realized in some utopian existence. The Church already exists as the spotless bride in Mary. At the same time Mary is the model for all Christians to imitate. She is the archetype of one who perfectly responds to mission. She becomes fully a person in saying 'yes' to her mission. So too each of us becomes a person by saying 'yes' to the unique mission which Christ proposes for us. As Balthasar puts it, the Church is always creative of persons, is always personalizing.

In large measure the philosophy of subjectivity which has dominated Western thinking in the last two hundred years is individualistic. In the centre stands the lonely individual with self-consciousness, self-knowledge and the lonely burden of freedom. The Austrian dialogical philosopher Ferdinand Ebner (1882–1931) says that modern thinking about the self is plagued by the isolation of the I (*Icheinsamkeit*). In Balthasar's vision of the Church, on the other hand, the I finds itself in communion with the Thou. The I is de-privatized. Christ, in calling each man or woman and in inserting him or her into the ecclesial community with a unique and irreplaceable mission, personalizes the subject. The subject is freed from isolation to find personhood in the community of the Church. The isolated I is overcome and the person becomes an *anima ecclesiastica*.

THE CHURCH OF LOVE, THE CHURCH OF OFFICE, THE CHURCH OF SINNERS

In having spoken of Mary and the feminine dimension of the Church we have already arrived at the centre of Balthasar's thinking about the Church, namely the Church of love. Balthasar believes that any merely sociological analysis of the Church is bound to miss the essence, namely the reality of love. And although he has a strong theology of the Church as institution, he firmly maintains that the institutional Church can only be understood within the perspective of the Church of love. Here Balthasar is fond of picking up Augustine's theme of the Church as *columba* or dove. Augustine appealed to the image of the beloved as the dove in Canticle of Canticles 2:13–14, 'Arise, my love, my fair one, and come away. O my dove, in the clefts of the rock, in the covert of the cliff, let me see your face, let me hear your voice, for your voice is sweet and your face is comely.' The dove, then, is the Church of love. For Balthasar, this Church of love, which is the innermost core of the Church, is most fully realized in Mary, but also in John, the disciple whom Jesus loved, the disciple whose head rested on the breast of Christ.

Within this Church of love is inserted the institutional Church symbolized in the figure of Peter. In speaking of the institutional Church, Balthasar once again appeals to his understanding of sexuality. The institutional Church is masculine. This is the Church governed by the ordained pastors whose task is to represent Christ before the community. In Balthasar's opinion Christ is masculine because he represents the Father's will to the world. Just as the man gives his seed in sexual intercourse, so Christ sows the seed of the Word and is a total outpouring of himself for his bride, the Church. The ordained members of the community, those who receive the office of representing Christ in the community, represent Christ in his masculine function. But the ordained are first and foremost baptized Christians. As the baptized they are feminine, they are receptive of Christ's grace, they must imitate Marian openness to the Word. Hence Peter has a subordinate role in regard to Mary. As regards authority, Mary stands under Peter. But as regards the essence of the Church, Peter must be inserted within the Marian Church. His institutional authority has no sense apart from the Church of love. In this sense, Balthasar would argue that in no way does woman have less in the Church. For woman represents the essence of what it means to be Church.

Finally we come to the idea of the Church as a community of sinners. On the one hand, we normally think of the Church as the communion of saints. We have already seen that the Church is holy. First of all, the institutional Church has the objective means of holiness and we saw above that subjective holiness has been perfectly realized in Mary. But, apart from Mary, the rest of Christ's flock consists of struggling sinners. Balthasar argues that Augustine did a certain amount of damage when he divided the Church neatly into the elect and the damned. For Augustine, the division between the saved and the damned has already taken place. But before the final judgement we must let the wheat and the tares grow together. The fullest consequence of this doctrine, thought through to its depth, would be that we cannot really pray for the false Church. All we can do is wait for the final revelation of God's judgement.

But Balthasar argues that such an approach fundamentally

destroys the nature of Christian solidarity. To be in the Church means to be in communion, and communion means solidarity. This in turn means that every gift or suffering which an individual Christian has can be of value for the others. No prayer or suffering ever goes unheeded. It can always bear some fruit in the Mystical Body. The French writer Léon Bloy (1846–1917) said that human freedom is like a flower whose seeds are blown by the wind to fructify mountains and valleys far off. He wrote, 'Every man who places an act of freedom, projects his personality into infinity . . . A deed of love, a striving of genuine compassion in its place sings the praise of God from Adam to the end of time, heals the sick, consoles the desperate, quiets the storm, liberates captives, converts unbelievers, protects entire humanity.'[4] Thus if sin is an act of isolation that never leads to genuine union, being in the Church of love inserts us into a solidarity that embraces the whole of creation. The Church is a great body of solidarity which stretches from the heights of holiness in Mary to the depths of God-forsakenness in the worst sinner. But no one is utterly abandoned, for those who have responded to the greater graces make intercession for those who are weak. As long as time persists, there is hope that even the man who has sunk into the lowest depths of human degradation will be saved because of the powerful intercession of his brothers and sisters in the Body of the Lord.

THE MYSTERY OF THE EUCHARIST

The Second Vatican Council declares 'The Liturgy is the summit toward which the activity of the Church is directed; at the same time it is the fountain from which all her power flows'.[5] Balthasar's theology of the eucharist can be seen as an attempt to unpack the richness which is contained in this conciliar affirmation. As we have seen, the eucharist is the culmination of the incarnation, for here Christ's bodiliness becomes available for the Christian. It is also the fulfilment of the work of the cross because here the fruits of the redemption are made available for God's people. And finally, the eucharist represents the culmination of anthropology, for in the eucharist men and women realize the highest dimension of freedom. They are incorporated into Christ's ascent to the Father. Exercising their participation in the sonship of Christ, their lives become an offering of thanksgiving to the Father. In the words of Gisbert Greshake, in the eucharist Christians live out the reality of 'gifted freedom'.[6]

Nonetheless, the reality of the eucharist raises a number of thorny questions for the believer and the theologian. Many of the questions centre around the problem of sacrifice. If Christ's sacrifice is perfect and is realized once and for all, in what sense is the Mass a sacrifice? If Christ has really done all that needs to be done, can we say that Christians actually *do* something in the Mass? Granted that Christians bring themselves as offering in the eucharist, can we say that they offer sacrifice? Indeed is the Father looking for sacrifice on the part of his people?

The first point that Balthasar makes in trying to respond to these questions is that we must always assign the priority in the eucharist to the action of Christ.[7] Only Christ is in a position to offer sacrifice. Our salvation depends on an action of God in Christ that in no way depends on our initiative. Christ has accomplished the redemption without asking for our consent. Thus the redemption of the human race is an objective fact. Balthasar stresses this point by appealing to 2 Corinthians 5:14, 'Since one has died, all have died'. We can in no way decide on the accomplishment of redemption. Because of Christ's death, and in a certain sense independently of our freedom, all have died. All we can do is ratify the decision God has made.

But if Christ alone offered the sacrifice of the cross, in what sense can this sacrifice be offered by the Church? For a first answer, Balthasar appeals to the work of Odo Casel.[8] Casel shows that with the resurrection Christ has become a life-giving Spirit. He can in the Spirit penetrate the depths of souls, touch them, and give them a share in his life. If on the cross he acted alone, in the eucharist he acts with the Church, and the Church is enabled to share actively in his sacrifice because she has his Spirit dwelling in her. Moreover, one can point to the Augustinian theology of the Body of Christ which we have already considered. The one who offers the sacrifice is the *Totus Christus*, that is, Christ the Head together with his members. All this is true, but Balthasar suggests that we must proceed with a certain caution, first of all, because the co-operation of the Christian in offering the sacrifice can never be compared to Christ's unique and unrepeatable experience on the cross. Only Christ entered into the full depths of God-forsakenness in bearing the sin of the world. The Christian is indeed invited to die with him, but the Christian's experience remains infinitely distant from the hell which Christ alone experienced. Secondly, Balthasar raises the question: how is the identity between Head and Members, between Bridegroom and Bride, achieved in such a way that the Christian is indeed able in Christ to offer sacrifice?

Part of the Catholic answer lies, to be sure, in the theology of the sacrament of priesthood. Since the Christian community is always a community of sinners, it can never measure up to the self-offering of Christ. But, as we saw when discussing Peter, Christ comes to the aid of human frailty and takes possession of people so that they can act in Christ's name. So the priest pronounces the words of consecration in the name of Christ. As Balthasar says, no man can dare to do this on his own authority. Christ must lay hold of him and take possession of his being.

But this answer as such is not sufficient, for the whole community of faith must be drawn into Christ's self-offering. Here Balthasar's returns to Mary and to the feminine dimension of faith. If we look at the life of Mary, we see that Christ pushes her away from him. He withdraws from Nazareth when he begins his public ministry and declares that association with him takes place not through the bonds of blood but by those of discipleship. In St Luke's eyes, Mary is the first and foremost of the disciples. She places herself under the Word of God and accepts to be placed apart. The final separation takes place under the cross. There she must say 'yes' to the death of her son. She must accept to be given away to John. Her faith costs her an ultimate renunciation. Thus, we see that Mary's activity, her co-involvement in the work of redemption, consists in the receptivity of faith. Just as in the annunciation, so in the cross, Mary cannot really *do* anything. She can only let it happen.

When we look at the sacrifice of Christ and Mary's participation in it, we find an overturning of the understanding of sacrifice as witnessed in the history of religions. Anthropologically considered, sacrifice is a human attempt to win something from God. The initiative lies with humankind. But Christ does not want to seize anything from the Father. As we saw in our treatment of Christology, Christ receives everything, especially his hour, from the Father's hands. And as we saw in the treatment of the paschal mystery, if until Good Friday Jesus is active in handing himself over, with Holy Saturday he experiences to the full the passivity of being disposed of by others. Mary participates in this oblation of Christ by her journey of faith to the cross where she must finally let go of Christ and let him go back to the Father. She does nothing but only says 'yes' to the fact that Jesus must die for her.

And here is the key to our participation in the sacrifice of Christ. In what sense do we offer with him? In what sense do we co-operate in the sacrifice of the Mass? The answer turns out to be a paradox. Our activity is the feminine receptivity of faith. The only thing that we can do is to say that we cannot do that which is necessary. All we can do is to say 'yes' to the fact that Christ must die for us. All we can do, in other words, is to let it happen. In the eucharist we bring to the Father our nothingness, our poverty, our lack of faith and lack of love, and in turn the Father gives us Christ, his faith and his love. This is the *admirabile commercium* (wonderful exchange) of which the Fathers of the Church speak. To be sure, such an attitude of faith demands that we actively enter into the sentiments of Christ. It is Christ alone who can offer the sacrifice, since he alone is the God-Man. But he draws us into his sacrifice as disciples. His sacrifice must become our sacrifice as we learn to follow his way, as we appropriate the attitude of the disciples and gradually learn to die to our egoism so that he can rise in us. Unless there is this openness to daily discipleship, the community's participation in the sacrifice of Christ becomes a contradiction and a blasphemy against Christ's gift of himself.

In the Old Testament the people of God offered a sacrifice of praise in the sense that they praised God for his glory and for his mighty deeds on behalf of his people. In what sense is the sacrifice of the Mass a sacrifice of praise? This question becomes especially important in view of the fact that the Reformers denied that the eucharist was a sacrifice, and in view of the declaration of the Council of Trent that the Mass is not merely a sacrifice of praise.[9] Here Balthasar tries to steer a middle course. It is well known that the Essene community of Qumran[10] did away with animal sacrifices and replaced these with a pure spiritual sacrifice. It is also true that the letter to the Hebrews speaks of 'offering up a sacrifice of praise to God, that is, the fruit of lips that acknowledge his name' (Heb 13:15). But the whole context of this passage in Hebrews is that Christians offer their sacrifice of praise through Jesus, that is, through the crucified and glorified Christ. The conclusion is that one cannot play off against one another the spiritual and the material. Our spiritual offering of praise is precisely the crucified Christ. The praise and the sacrifice are two sides of one reality. In other words, our praise of the Father consists in our inserting ourselves into the sacrifice of Christ, whose thanksgiving to the Father consisted in his willingness to let himself be offered for the sake of his people.

Finally, we could mention that the sign that the sacrifice is accepted is the fact that the Father gives us back the Son to be consumed in the holy communion. Here we see again that the sacrifice and the meal form two sides of one total mystery. The meal is the completion of the sacrifice and the realization of all God's saving dealings with his people. For, from the beginning, God has wanted nothing other than union with humankind. The goal of all his actions has been nothing other than the marriage of heaven and earth. In the eucharist this purpose is fulfilled, for the eucharist is the wedding feast of the Lamb (Rev 19:9). In the eucharistic banquet there is true communion between God and humanity.

We conclude this section by noting that the eucharist is also the supreme moment of action and contemplation. The eucharist is action because the Mass makes present the event where Christ hands himself over to the Father. Christ alone is the High Priest who can offer the sacrifice. As we have seen, his action involves our action, but the action of the Christian community never becomes a 'work' in the Lutheran sense.[11] Our action consists in letting Christ act in us. At the same time the eucharist is contemplation, for Christ's action can never be adequately grasped or appropriated. The believer can never, so to say, catch up with what Christ has done. And this fact grounds the possibility and indeed the necessity of eucharistic adoration. Christ's action in his self-giving unto death remains so full that his presence perdures. Christ never takes back the gift. The body once given remains. And we, the faithful, cannot but bend the knee in wondering adoration before the mystery,[12] trying to grasp the infinite depth of the love, and begging that in some small measure our lives might begin to correspond to the mystery we contemplate.

Notes

1 See 'Who is the Church?' in *Church and World* (New York: Sheed and Ward, 1967), pp. 112–65.

2 The terms form and matter are to be understood within the perspective of Aristotle's metaphysics. According to this tradition every being in our experience is constituted by the two principles of form and matter. A statue, for example, is made of marble (the matter) but is given the shape of David (the form) by Michelangelo. These principles of matter and form were applied by St Thomas and other theologians to help explain various realities of faith. Thus it was said that each sacrament had matter and form. In baptism, for example, the matter is water and the form is given by the words used in administering the sacrament.

3 This phrase in Latin can be understood as the prolongation of Christ in the world.

4 Léon Bloy, *Le Désespéré* (ed. Bollery-Petit) (1964), p. 113 as cited by Balthasar, *Theodramatik* III (Einsiedeln: Johannes, 1980), p. 386.

5   *Sacrosanctum Concilium*, no. 10.

6   See *Libertà Donata* (Brescia: Queriniana, 1984).

7   For Balthasar's theology of the eucharist, and in particular his under-
    standing of eucharistic sacrifice, see 'Die Messe, ein Opfer der
    Kirche?' in *Spiritus Creator* (Einsiedeln: Johannes, 1967), pp. 166–
    217; also *Theodramatik* III, pp. 363–79.

8   Odo Casel (1886–1948) was a Benedictine monk of the Maria Laach
    abbey in Germany. He was a noted liturgist who developed the theo-
    logy of the liturgy as the re-enactment of the mysteries of Christ.

9   See Council of Trent, Session XXII, chapter 9, canon 3 (DS 1753).

10 The Essenes were a Jewish sect living in Palestine at the time of the
    ministry of Jesus. Their origins date back roughly to the second cen-
    tury BC and they died out around the second century AD. They were
    noted for their asceticism and communistic life-style and had a piety
    resembling that of the Pharisees.

11 Luther taught that the Christian was saved by the grace of Christ alone
    and not by human works. Since Balthasar argues that in the eucharist
    it is really Christ who acts and we merely let him act in us, this
    approach respects Luther's concern to give the priority to Christ's
    grace in everything.

12 For a small meditation on Balthasar's understanding of eucharistic
    adoration see 'The veneration of the Holy of Holies' in *Elucidations*
    (London: SPCK, 1975), pp. 119–25.

11

The Christian states of life

INTRODUCTION

One of Balthasar's central convictions is that love alone is credible. If love plays the central role in Balthasar's theology in general, the same is true for his theology of vocation, and in his book *The Christian State of Life*, he notes that if his presentation of the theology of vocation has any merit of originality, it lies in seeking to understand the mystery of vocation from the standpoint of love.

The first point we observe is that the common destiny of every person and especially of every Christian is that of love. God has elected us and called us to this vocation in Christ. As St Paul puts it, 'He destined us in love to be his sons through Jesus Christ' (Eph 1:5). This means that every baptized person is called to love without limits, or in other words, to the fullness of perfection. There can be no question of dividing the states of life according to greater or lesser degrees of love. The second observation which Balthasar makes is that every genuine love has the form of a vow. Lovers wish to pledge themselves, to bestow themselves upon the beloved, and they wish to make this gift of themselves in a way which says 'forever'. But if the human being is called to love, and if this is the vocation of all, then how can we account for the diversity of the states of life?

FROM THE PRIMEVAL STATE TO THE DIVISION OF THE STATES

To answer our question, we must introduce a number of themes. First of all, there is the fact of sin. Because sin has entered the world, the ordinary man or woman is not inclined to make a total gift of self to God. Moreover, one can understand this fact better if one looks at the original state and at what happened to that state with the fall of Adam. By the original state, Balthasar understands the human condition of integrity as God intended it in paradise. How should we understand this original state of integrity? Balthasar takes as his point of departure the evangelical counsels, since they represent for him the fullness of self-giving implied in love. From this point of view the state of integrity in paradise can be understood as the union of poverty and riches, obedience and freedom, virginity and fecundity. Let us look at each of these in turn.

The key to obedience and freedom can be seen in Christ's Sonship. His whole being consists in fulfilling the Father's will, and yet this is no alien obedience but the obedience of Sonship. In Jesus we see that autonomy and theonomy are not contradictories. Finding one's freedom in God's will is the meaning of human integrity as God foresaw it in paradise.

As regards poverty, Balthasar cites the remark of St John Chrysostom, 'The chilling expression "mine and thine" did not exist in those days'.[1] All the Fathers are agreed that there was no private property in the original state. There was no need for such an institution, for no threat existed among human beings. God intended that each person's riches be put at the service of others.

The most difficult point is the integrity found in the union of virginity and fecundity. Once again it is important to note that the point of departure must be Christological. In Christ we see a virginal life which issues forth in an infinite fecundity on the cross. The same integrity is realized in Mary. She was a virgin but through God's call she become the mother of God. In light of this restoration of God's original plan, Balthasar argues with the Fathers that, in the original state, man and woman were called simultaneously to virginity and to fecundity. He admits that we cannot *imagine* how this could have been. For Balthasar, what is important to affirm is the triple assertion: first, that God created man and woman to be sexually differentiated; secondly, that their sexual union was not like ours today since sexual intercourse today is always marked by some degree of egoism and by death; and thirdly, that their union was meant to be fruitful.

With the fall of Adam this original plan of God was ruined. Man and woman are born today without this original integrity. The human vocation which should have been a pure self-giving of love according to the evangelical counsels is no longer possible in the form God intended. What should have been a wholly positive gift is now rendered difficult by concupiscence and selfishness. The gates of paradise were closed by sin. Only the cross was able to reopen them, but this implies that the way back to paradise must now be by a detour. The way of love will imply the way of renunciation. In short, what in paradise was a single, undivided vocation has now given way to diverse states of life, all of which in some way reflect the original plan, but do so now under the broken conditions of sinfulness.

Balthasar has thus shown that a first condition for understanding the division of the states of life is the introduction of the reality of sin in the world through the fall. But there is another point which is of critical importance. This point Balthasar learned from the *Spiritual Exercises* of St Ignatius where, in the second week, Ignatius helps the exercitant to be open to the unpredictable mission offered by the sovereign freedom of God. The *Exercises* unfold the drama of divine and human freedom. The vocation which I have is never merely a question of human desire or of rational planning. Ultimately human freedom must await the divine call. Thus, even the man or woman who feels drawn to a perfect act of abandonment through the evangelical counsels may not be called to the religious life. Ultimately, the critical motive for the choice of a state of life is the divine decision.

THE STATE OF ELECTION

As should already be clear, the impulse lying behind Balthasar's reflections on the states of life is his desire to bring into relief the life of the evangelical counsels. Hence the weight of his reflection falls on the state of election. Before proceeding to present Balthasar's ideas about the elected state, we should make clear that for him election implies a twofold possibility, that of the religious life and that of the priesthood. Although a person may be called to one or the other or both, it is important to see priesthood and religious life as two sides of a single election. These two sides of election have an inner dynamism toward each other.

What is the core of the call to the religious life? Balthasar begins his reflection with a consideration of discipleship in the New Testament. The gospels are full of encounters between Jesus and persons in need. One of the most striking features of these encounters is that Jesus touches the person's life and then sends him or her away. He is sent back into everyday life, transformed by the encounter, perhaps called to spread abroad his faith in Jesus and to give praise to God. Sometimes a person healed by Jesus, such as the Gerasene demoniac, wants to remain with Jesus, but Jesus does not give his permission. In Mark 5 we read 'The man who had been possessed with demons begged Jesus that he might be with him. But Jesus refused and said to him, "Go home to your friends, and tell them how much the Lord has done for you, and how he has had mercy on you" ' (vv. 18–19)

It is otherwise, however, with the disciples. There it is Jesus who makes the offer. Indeed it is a command. The choice lies with him. He wants a particular person to be with him, to follow him, to go where he goes. Once the invitation has been offered, the one called must respond immediately, without conditions. Jesus once spoke of himself as having nowhere to lay his head (Matt 8:20). Jesus is an itinerant, he goes according to the will of the Father to preach the Kingdom. There is never time to rest, for the time is short and the mission urgent. The one called to discipleship is summoned to this homelessness, or rather his home is only in Jesus. The only important thing is to be with him.

If the disciple is to follow Jesus wherever he goes, then this implies that he must follow him even to the cross. The disciple is the one who understands the mystery of Jesus's identity, who understands that his way must be the way of the cross. We have already seen that the paschal mystery stands in the centre of Balthasar's theology. Jesus is born in order to die. If God has seen the creation from all eternity in light of his Son, the cross was not a possibility envisaged with the creation. The cross is seen from all eternity but as the result of sin. If, during his ministry, the Son of Man has no place to call his own, on the cross he is lifted up from the earth and, so to say, cast out from the creation. According to the letter to the Hebrews, Jesus dies outside the holy city (Heb 13:12). Indeed the cross represents the non-place, the 'outside' *par excellence*. Being made sin, Jesus is cast out from the earth. His place is the no-place. He is radically forsaken by God and by man.

The call to the religious life is thus the call to this intimate form of discipleship. It is so total an abandonment of self that the man or woman who professes the evangelical counsels chooses to have no other dwelling place than in Christ. Moreover, it is the choice of existence in the cross. The religious realizes that there is no way back to the paradise except the path that leads through the cross. He or she seeks the original integration of the paradise state, but is willing to do so under the form of renunciation. Religious life is the reverse mirror-image of the Garden of paradise. It is integration refounded under the form of negation. The centre of this commitment lies in obedience where the religious rejects autonomy in order like Christ to have no other food than the will of the Father (see John 4:34). The consecrated person, moreover, seeks virginity surrendering bodily union with another for the greater spiritual fruitfulness of the Mystical Body. Finally, like Christ, religious do not consider riches a thing to be grasped but empty themselves allowing the Lord to complete them with his infinite fullness.

CHRISTIAN PRIESTHOOD

We noted in the previous section that in Balthasar's theology the life of the counsels and the life of the priesthood form one state of election. Let us try to understand how this is so by examining first the nature of Christ's priesthood, then the ministerial priesthood of the ordained, and finally the reciprocity between priesthood and the evangelical counsels.

The first point which we note is that Christ's priesthood is an existential priesthood which consists in the offer of himself to the Father in love. What is offered is not the blood of animals but his own obedience. Moreover, there is no attempt on the part of the man Jesus Christ to win something from God or to change his mind. The self-offering of Christ is the response of Jesus to the Father's desire to save. All the initiative proceeds from the Father. In the sacrifice of Christ there is a perfect unity between the person who offers and what is offered, for Christ offers nothing less than himself. And since he is the God-man, his sacrifice is unsurpassable.

One might ask why there is a need for a ministerial priesthood in the Church if Christ has fulfilled the Old Testament prefigurements of sacrifice. Balthasar responds to this question in two steps. First, he reflects upon the nature of Christ's office as priest. We have already seen that the cross is Jesus's supreme act of love for the Father. But on the cross the feeling of love is absent. Rather Jesus cries out on the cross in a sense of abandonment. The loving face of the Father is hidden. In Gethsemane and on the cross Jesus is confronted with the naked reality of the Father's will which he must accept in blind obedience. In this sense the sacrifice of Christ is expressed with a radically objective character. In Balthasar's words, it has all the marks of an institutional act.

The next step is to see that just as the Father manifested his will in an objective, institutional way, so Christ can and does demand of Christians an obedience which mirrors his own. In this context Balthasar situates the ministerial priesthood. Just as the Father is represented to the world in Jesus, so Jesus is represented to the world in the ministerial priesthood. The bishop and the priest have the function of summoning their people to obedience in Christ. This obedience can at times take on the same form of 'not seeing' as Jesus's obedience did in Gethsemane and on Calvary.

Moreover, the nature of this institutional priesthood becomes clearer when one realizes that the world we live in is permeated by sinfulness. Not all the baptized in Christ are fired with the love which leads to a total abandonment of self to Christ. Many must be led along by a holy fear and thus be brought gradually to the surrender of love. For these Christians obedience is especially necessary.

Finally, Balthasar notes that it is essential for the salvation of the world that Christ continue to be present to the world. He does this through his Word, his sacraments and the ministerial priesthood. Since no human being is able to represent Christ adequately, and since the world's salvation absolutely depends on such a representation, Christ takes hold of a man and through his sacramental grace enables that man to represent him. No human being is able to do this, and thus there is always a yawning gap between the priest and his office. The subjective holiness of the priest never matches the objective representation of his office, but nevertheless Christ guarantees that when the priest acts in his name by preaching his word and celebrating his sacraments he is present to the faithful with his grace through the action of the priest.

Thus far in our exposition of ministerial priesthood we have concentrated on the necessity of a priesthood in the Church. In this sense we have been reflecting on the function of the priest. And Balthasar would indeed put the emphasis on the objective ministerial role of the priest. If the evangelical counsels represent primarily the subjective surrender of the consecrated person to Christ, the priesthood emphasizes his objective office in the community. Still these two aspects cannot be played off against one another. On the one hand, the subjective surrender of the religious to Christ becomes objective as he or she is inserted into a religious family with a rule approved by the Church. One thinks of the great founders of religious orders such as Francis of Assisi or Ignatius of Loyola who submitted their rule to the pope. On the other hand, the objective ministry of the priest calls for a way of life in conformity with the ministry, a way of life that makes the ministry credible. The long tradition of the Church has thus seen an inner connaturality between the priesthood and the evangelical counsels. In the Western Church, through the vow of celibacy and the promise of obedience to the bishop and through the summons to simplicity of life, the priest's existence is shaped according to the spirit of the evangelical counsels.[2]

The relationship between objective and subjective holiness, between what is and what ought to be is expressed beautifully in the three symbolic figures of the New Testament: Mary, Peter, and John. Mary, with her perfect 'yes' to the will of God, expresses in her whole life the integrity of paradise lost with the fall. Moreover, we can say that she represents the perfect example of the existential priesthood, namely the perfect correspondence between person and office, where all is ordered to the divine mission. According to Balthasar, the religious life is represented by the figure of St John, the disciple whom Jesus loved, the friend who lays his head on the breast of Christ. With Mary, John represents the Church of love which comes to expression most perfectly in the evangelical counsels.

But to understand the full reality of the Church, we must place Mary and John alongside of Peter. Balthasar meditates upon the gospel scene, where after receiving the news of the Lord's resurrection, John and Peter both run to the empty tomb. John, as a symbol of the Church of love, arrives first but he gives the precedence to Peter. Thus the Church of love does not shy from submission to the institutional Church. But equally important is the other gospel scene where the Lord confronts Peter three times with the question: 'Do you love me?' (see John 21:15ff.). Peter is to be installed as pastor of Christ's Church on earth with supreme responsibility and authority to bind and loose. But he cannot be given this office until he makes his triple declaration of love. The Church of office has no other function than to serve the Church of love. As Balthasar says, office in the Church is meant to be the crystallization of love.

LAY PERSONS IN THE CHURCH

Perhaps the most important thing to be said about every baptized person is that he or she, as Paul would put it, has been called out of darkness into Christ's light (see Col 1:12–13). In other words, the fundamental division, prior to that of elected state and lay state, is that of the separation between the reign of sin and the Kingdom of Christ. Every Christian is summoned to share in Christ's reign. This means, for Balthasar, that he or she is invited to participate in God's own life. In every baptized lay man or woman, God's plan for the world is fulfilled: namely, the union he desires between himself and humankind, the divine *connubium*. This involves, as we have already seen, an unmistakable call to love without reserve. Moreover, it is clear that Christ has a mission for each man and woman, a mission unique to that person, necessary for the building up of his reign. In responding to that mission, the Christian becomes a person.

From the point of view of the institutional Church it would seem that the pastors are active and the lay persons passive. If it is true that certain aspects of the Church's life belong primarily to the pastors, such as the celebration of the sacraments, it is by no means true that the laity are merely passive. First of all, certain sacraments such as baptism and marriage are or can be administered by the laity. Secondly, there are other important ministries in the Church such as that of catechist which are open to the laity.

But even more important is the fact that in the spiritual life there is never room for passivity. If, as we have seen, the Church's being is primarily feminine, the feminine reception of the seed is anything but sheer passivity. Rather the woman's role is a highly active receptivity. Without this active receptivity the seed would not gestate. So it is with the Christian in his or her listening to the Word of God and reception of the sacraments. The lay person is called to a supremely active assimilation of the work of Christ through the minister. As Balthasar puts it, 'One who is merely passive does not really receive: to possess, one must accept; and the more spiritual the gift, the more gratefully and happily it should be accepted. Thus the reception of grace becomes automatically an action—an action that accepts, takes hold of, understands, executes, and transmits.'[3]

But if it is true that lay persons are not passive in regard to the sacraments, they are revealed as supremely active in their life in the world. For it is important to recall that the sacraments do not exist for their own sake. Indeed, the institutional Church exists to help

Christians realize their existential priesthood, that is, the praise of the Lord with the sacrifice of a Christian's entire being in the midst of the world.

This means, firstly, reflecting in the midst of the world, the possibility of the reintegration of what was lost in paradise. For example, the Christian knows how to use material things, even wealth, without becoming a slave to them. Again, the Christian lay man or woman gives his body in love to the spouse in marriage, thus demonstrating that *eros* can be transfigured into *caritas*. Finally Christians submit in obedience to the will of Christ within the institutional Church without losing their freedom of sonship.

Again we must stress the reality of mission. The baptized man or woman is not called to be a cleric. The clericalization of the laity would be a terrible distortion of the dignity of the Christian. Rather, the lay man or woman is called to bear witness to the values of Christ in the midst of the secular world where he or she is placed. They are called to sanctify the earth, to render it human, open to God's redeeming action. Christians are thus called to posit signs and anticipations of the reign of God wherever they build the human city in the midst of their work and recreation. They do all this with hope and, as Marcel often repeated, hope is never passive. But, at the same time, Christians realize that their actions as such will never produce the Kingdom of God, for we live in a world where Christ still struggles with the power of evil, where we still await the final overthrowing of the last enemy, death. In this situation, which Balthasar does not hesitate to call apocalyptic, Christians recognize that all their activity must be carried on under the sign of the cross. Hence they must be prepared for persecution and even martyrdom. Thus, their life in the world will be poised between hope and action, labour for the Kingdom and evangelical patience, vigilance and struggle. To be sure, God calls them to collaborate in the struggle against evil and injustice, but the Christian knows that the victory belongs to the Lord alone and not to human efforts.

CHRISTIAN MARRIAGE

We have seen that the essence of vocation according to Balthasar is the call to love and that every genuine love takes the form of a vow. In this context it is obvious that Christian matrimony is a state of life, for here a man and a woman bind themselves together by vow and pledge themselves to each other in Christ forever.

The ultimate background for Balthasar's understanding of marriage are the trinitarian processions. Balthasar has always sought to understand the Trinity as a community of love. He follows the tradition of Richard of St Victor (d. 1173) according to which the human analogy of friendship provides the best model for understanding God's trinitarian being. In this tradition, when two people love one another, their union is an example of *amor mutuus*, but if such a love is not to be closed in on itself and hence become a subtle form of self-seeking, it must open to a third whom Richard of St Victor calls the *condilectus* (co-beloved). The best example of this *amor consummatus* is the conjugal love of husband and wife which blossoms in their child. Hence matrimonial love becomes an image of the Trinity, reflecting the love of the Father and the Son which overflows in the Holy Spirit.

Here we note as well the theme of the fruitfulness of love. Balthasar's approach is radically personalist. The goal of marriage is not that of producing children. Rather the purpose of marriage is the self-donation of the partners in love. But Balthasar argues that there is never self-donation without fruitfulness. In marriage the fruitfulness which is most visible and concrete is the bodily fruitfulness which is the sign of the fecundity of the love of the couple. In a striking reflection Balthasar notes the surprise element of this fruitfulness. Fecundity can never be planned but must be awaited as gift. The arrival of the child is the sign that the union of the spouses was far more fruitful than they could have imagined.

The other dimension of Christian matrimony is the christological. In Ephesians 5, Paul points out how Christian marriage has its foundation in the surrender of Christ to his spouse, the Church, on the cross. Christ gives himself eucharistically to the Church. He pledges his body totally for her. The Church, on the other hand, is feminine receptivity to accept the seed of his Word and to let this seed become spiritually fruitful in her. In Christian marriage, in their sexual intercourse, the man and the woman act out symbolically the reciprocal love of Christ and the Church. The man gives his seed, but this biological giving is a sacramental sign of self-donation to his wife. The wife is receptive, but this receptivity toward her husband is no sign of an alien obedience, rather it is the receptivity of self-surrender. Balthasar would say that the role of the spouses has a certain order, even a certain super-ordination and sub-ordination. Paul says, for example, that the husband is head of the wife. But this ordering of the relationship cannot be understood according to the pattern of the master–slave relationship. Christ has abolished every

sort of relating according to exploitation. Rather, the superordina-
tion and sub-ordination of marriage has to be understood in Christ,
that is, the role of the sexes remains distinct and irreversible, but at
the same time, there is a new equality of the sexes brought about by
Christ's transvaluation of values. The Christian understanding of
marriage is that of equality in differentiation.

THE COMPLEMENTARITY OF THE STATES OF LIFE

It is clear that what stands closest to Balthasar's heart is the elected
state and in particular the life of the evangelical counsels, for they
represent the most perfect concretizations of love which we can
realize on earth. Nonetheless Balthasar is clear that both the elected
state and the married state are necessary for the realization of the
Church's mission.

The lay state, represented most clearly by the married, represents
the Church's insertion in the world. These are the Christians, so to
say, on the front line between the kingdom of light and the kingdom
of darkness. But if they represent the mission of the Church, the
religious represent the heart beat of the Church, for they symbolize
the burning centre of love. One image to express the harmony
between the two states is the contraction and the expansion of the
heart muscle.[4] In the religious, the heart of the Church contracts to
its centre. But the contraction exists for the sake of the expansion, so
that the blood which carries life can be transmitted to all parts of the
body.

The other image is that of the tree which extends from its crown
down to its deepest roots.[5] As Balthasar puts it, the broader the
crown of the tree, the deeper must be its roots. In other words, the
mission of the Church, especially that of the laity, will be more
efficacious and have wider impact, the more that the work of the
Church is rooted in her depths, that is, in the life of love symbolized
by the evangelical counsels. Hence, as Paul says, all the members of
the Body of Christ with their different charisms exist in an organic
relation to one another. No one state of life can exist without the
others, but in the providence of God, each state of life completes the
others to build up the Body of Christ in a mutual harmony which
serves to make the Church the light for the nations.

Notes

1 *The Christian State of Life* (San Francisco: St Ignatius Press, 1983), p. 109.

2 As recently as the Second Vatican Council, the intrinsic link between the call to priesthood and life according to the spirit of the evangelical counsels has been emphasized. See *Presbyterorum Ordinis*, nos 15–17.

3 Balthasar, op. cit., p. 337.

4 See ibid., p. 347.

5 See ibid., p. 348.

12

Trinity and history

THE ENIGMA OF THE FINITE

We have seen in Chapter 2 that at the centre of Balthasar's theological project is the mystery of Being, and that he approaches this mystery from the perspective of the transcendental properties of Being: the One, the True, the Good and the Beautiful. As early as 1947, Balthasar explored for the first time at length the philosophical question of truth. This work was later incorporated into Balthasar's trilogy as the first volume of *Theologik*.

In what sense can we and must we speak of Being as true? In Balthasar's meditation upon this question we see a certain influence of Heidegger with his idea that truth is an unveiling, an event in which Being manifests itself. If this is the case, then it follows that truth is always an event which involves freedom. The event of truth presupposes that Being discloses itself. At the same time, for this event to happen, subjects must open themselves in freedom to this self-disclosure. Already we see here in Balthasar's thinking the mutual interpenetration of truth and love. There is no event of truth without a mutual self-surrender. Balthasar writes:

The meaning of Being lies in love, and knowledge is only explainable through love and for love. The will which exists in the object to open itself and the will which exists in the knowing subject to open itself in receptivity are the double form of the surrender which manifests itself in these two ways. From this follows the insight that love is never separable from the truth. Just as little as there could be knowledge without the will, so also truth is hardly knowable without love.[1]

But how are we to conceive this relationship between knowledge and love? How are we to conceive this self-disclosure of Being? If we remain within a Heideggerian perspective we will say that Being itself is finite, and that the event of its self-manifestation is the meaning of temporality. Being and time are correlative. Time is the unfolding of Being. But does Heidegger not too quickly dispose of the dialectic between the finite and the infinite? When *Dasein* as human being-in-the-world becomes aware of its finitude, does it not in its transcendence open out to the mystery of Infinite Being? Perhaps then Hegel is correct when he sees the finite as the expression of the Infinite. Hegel too tries to do justice to the mystery of the temporality of Being and he sees time as the self-expression of the Absolute. For Hegel the mystery of Being is the mystery of subjectivity. The ultimate ground of reality is the Absolute Subject who, however, in order to become concrete freedom, must posit an other as the mediation of his Absolute Self-Consciousness.

For Hegel too the Mystery of Being is the Mystery of self-revelation. For his idealistic philosophy as well, the fundamental philosophical question is the relation between truth and love. But Balthasar asks whether Hegel does justice to the mystery of love. The point at issue is the relationship between the I and the Thou and the meaning of freedom. Hegel realizes that the I always remains an abstraction apart from involvement with the other. And indeed he has some beautiful reflections on the meaning of friendship. But in the end one could ask whether Hegel ever does full justice to the reality of the other. Is the other loved for his or her own sake or is the other ultimately a means for the I's achieving its realization? If God is the Absolute I, does this mean that the world is necessary to him for coming to consciousness of himself? Does the eternal need time in order to be? Balthasar would argue that Hegel's solution is inadequate in that he absorbs love in knowledge. According to Balthasar, in Hegel's system reason prevails over freedom. Love becomes a logical necessity.

If for Balthasar love is the meaning of Being, then a better starting point for understanding Being would be interpersonal relationships. Here we can pursue this point as regards the question of truth. We have seen that truth is the self-disclosure of Being. But this self-disclosure never happens in isolation. It always involves a community of persons. Human being-in-the world is always being-together.

As regards this interpersonal dimension of Being, Balthasar finds great inspiration in the Austrian philosopher Ferdinand Ebner.[2] Ebner deplored a fundamental weakness in modern culture since Descartes, namely the isolation of the I. He called the crisis of modern culture 'the loneliness of the I' (*Icheinsamkeit*). The I is cut off from others and dreams of breaking out of its isolation but does not know how.

Fundamentally the I cannot break out of its isolation by its own efforts. Rather the I must let itself be gifted with the other. And indeed there is a phenomenon of everyday experience where this giftedness takes place, namely in the experience of language. Everyday we do succeed in communicating, and we do this through language. Yet language is never something we create out of nothing. No one invents language on their own. In the first instance language is received as a gift, even if, once the gift is received, human persons can modify their language with an almost infinite creativity.

The primordial enigma of language is that the I does not have in itself the resources to reach the other. And yet the miracle of communication happens. Ebner believes that the fact of language means that the essence of the human consists in having the word. The person does not create this word. It is given. The word links the I to the Thou and makes communication possible. Philosophers can point to the phenomenon of the word and of dialogue, but they cannot explain it. Ebner argues that there is no naturalistic explanation of language. The fact of language points to a transcendent source. If people are able to speak, this is because they participate in the Logos which transcends them. For Ebner, then, there are three fundamental realities in human communication: the I, the Thou, and the word which binds them together. Often he calls the word 'the between' (*das zwischen*) which is the bond of union. Although Ebner works on a purely philosophical level, one sees that his interpretation of human dialogue points in the direction of the Trinity. He comes fairly close to a trinitarian model of dialogue.

A reflection on the meaning of Being thus points us in the direction of self-disclosure. Truth happens when Being reveals itself. In finite experience this self-disclosure comes to expression in language. And as another philosopher of dialogue, Franz Rosenzweig, has shown, every uttering of the word requires time. So Being reveals itself in time. But can we content ourselves with Heidegger's analysis of the finite self-unfolding of Being or even with Hegel's dialectical understanding of Infinite Being's self-expression in time? If Heidegger fails to take into account the infinite and Hegel reduces the infinite to logic thereby surrendering the mystery of freedom, the experience of human dialogue points us toward a deeper approach in the mystery of love. So, as always, Balthasar would argue that the path from below is doomed to failure. We must begin again from above in the mystery of trinitarian love. Only in the Trinity do we see the true interpenetration of knowledge and love, of Logos and Spirit, which makes possible the mystery of revelation and gives us the needed key for unlocking the mystery of our human existence in time and history.

THE TRINITY AS COMMUNITY OF LOVE

Like many contemporary theologians Balthasar stresses that the economic Trinity is rooted in the immanent Trinity. Hence what we learn of the Trinity in history gives us the key to understanding the divine life. Being inspired by Johannine theology, Balthasar finds an opening to an understanding of the Trinity in the fourth evangelist's affirmation: 'God so loved the world that he gave his only-begotten Son' (John 3:16). If the relation of Father and Son in the incarnation is one of love, this is because in the divine life, the procession of the Son from the Father is a procession of love. Hence Balthasar seeks to understand the inner life of the divine Trinity strictly in terms of love. Here he breaks out of the model of St Thomas according to which the first procession should be understood as an intellectual act in the way that the word of the mind is produced from an act of understanding and the second procession is to be likened to an act of the will whereby the Holy Spirit unites the Word to the Father who utters it.

Balthasar rather feels more drawn to the tradition of St Bonaventure (c. 1217–74) and Richard of St Victor. According to Bonaventure, the procession of the Word is a procession of love and takes place *per modum exemplaritatis* (in the manner of an image). The Son, being the perfect expression of the Father and being also the perfect response to his love, is the image of the Father both in the immanent Trinity and in the economy of salvation. The Father gives everything he has to the Son, but still this self-giving does not exhaust the Father's capacity to give, namely with the Son. Here Balthasar follows the example of Bonaventure and argues that the second procession, that of the Holy Spirit, takes place *per modum liberalitatis* (in the manner of generosity).[3]

What is the best human analogy that can help us to understand the

142

inner-trinitarian life? The Augustinian–Thomistic tradition appeals to the mind with its internal acts of knowing and loving. Balthasar prefers the model suggested by Richard of St Victor, namely that of ecstatic love. In the third book of his *De Trinitate*, Richard appeals to the model of communion to illumine the mystery of the Trinity. In order to have the communion of love there is required a lover and a beloved. Hence if God is love, there must be in God at least two persons. A human person would not be an adequate partner for God's love, for no human person could adequately respond to his love. God seeks a partner worthy of himself. But at the same time, if the love of the two divine persons remained closed in upon itself, it would be a type of mutual egoism. Our human experience reveals that true love opens out beyond itself. When I love another person, I want to share that love with a third person. Richard of St Victor thus sees the third person of the Trinity as the *condilectus*, the mutually beloved of the Father and the Son.

Balthasar stands firmly in this tradition. For him the most adequate human analogy for the trinitarian life is conjugal love. Human marriage should never be understood in a functional sense. The value of marriage is strictly personal. The gaze of the lover is focused one hundred per cent on the beloved. But love always contains a fecundity far greater than the lovers themselves can imagine. Hence in conjugal love the sexual self-giving of the spouses, even if it is wholly oriented to the other, often blossoms forth in a new life. The appearance of the child comes as a surprise, as the sign of the ever-greater fruitfulness of their love. In the same way, in the trinitarian life, the love of Father and Son opens out to the Holy Spirit. The Spirit is at one and the same time the bond of their union and the opening of their love beyond the Godhead. With Walter Kasper, Balthasar could say that the Spirit represents the ecstatic character of the divine life.[4] The divine love is not closed in upon itself but is an open love, open to the world, to time and to history.

The key then to our understanding of the meaning of the world, of time and of history is the Trinity. Balthasar notes that outside of God there is nothing. Where then does the world have its place? Balthasar would argue that the world exists within the Trinity, in the infinite open space between the divine persons. The procession of the Spirit indicates God's opening to time and history. The procession of the Son implies that he is the archetype to which the creation is called to conform. If then we ask what is the sense of our time and our history, the answer must ultimately be sought in the

Trinity from which the world comes forth and to which it is called to return.

CHRIST THE FULLNESS OF TIME

According to Balthasar, the sense of history can only be found in Christ. Christ's coming is the turning point of human history, the hinge on which time revolves. In him history has reached the fulfilment destined for it by God. The time from his incarnation to his ascension, therefore, represents the fullness of time.

In theological language one would say that Christ is the *eschaton*. History has reached its end in the sense of arriving at its *telos* (goal). But how should we understand the relationship between Christ's eschatological time and chronological time? In Balthasar's view the two are incommensurable. One cannot measure the former by the latter. As Balthasar puts it, the new aeon cannot be added on to the old one, but originates from it incommensurably as from a right angle.[5] Here we are touching upon a problem already hinted at in Chapter 2 when we talked about catholicity, namely the relationship between the vertical and the horizontal. From one point of view, the fullness of time must be understood vertically. The Logos descends from heaven and becomes flesh. But Balthasar warns that the vertical dimension is not in opposition to the horizontal. It is equally true that Christ is fully embedded in the process of history, especially the history of Israel.

In this context Balthasar offers a number of interesting reflections. If we look at the history of the world, we can see, as certain philosophers such as Karl Jaspers (1883–1969) have pointed out,[6] that a decisive turn took place in the several hundred years before the birth of Christ, namely the transition from *mythos* to *logos*.[7] The emergence of the great Greek philosophers such as Plato and Aristotle indicates the breakthrough to reason. Jaspers calls this the beginning of axial time. When Jaspers attempts to understand the meaning of history, he makes an appeal to open reason. Reason is precisely openness to the universal. According to Jaspers the human person is transcendence, called to move beyond to the ever wider horizon of the Encompassing.[8] Within time there are ciphers that point to God but no historical event can ever claim to be the definitive manifestation of God's presence in time. Such a claim would block transcendence and contradict open reason.

Balthasar would agree that it is significant that Christ is born precisely in this moment of breakthrough for the human race. But he would argue that God has made use of this turning point for his own purposes. The coming of the eschatological event does not annul the progress of human history. Rather God works within these events to bring about an unexpected fulfilment from above. Jesus is fully embedded within history but gradually his presence comes ever more to the centre of the stage, all other figures with their claims to absoluteness recede into the background. His uniqueness stands out before all the others.[9] This uniqueness is especially seen in his claim to be the way, the truth and the life, a claim unheard of in human history. If other founders of the religions claimed to offer a way, Jesus claims to be *the* way.

Of critical importance in the preparation for Christ's coming is God's election of Israel to be his covenant partner. Jesus cannot be understood apart from Israel. He is Jewish to the depths of his being. But it is equally true that Israel cannot be understood apart from the Christ. Israel's whole history is a dynamic propulsion toward a fulfilment which it can never reach on its own. Only God can fulfil his promise from above. Israel embodies in a dramatic way the dialogue between God and man. The more God offers his friendship, the more Israel manifests a hardness of heart and rejects his covenant love. Balthasar meditates at length on the problem of the meaning of Israel's existence in the time after Christ. On the one hand, he would agree that God remains ever faithful. Hence God does not turn his back on Israel. On the other hand, as St Paul says, the fulfilment of all God's promises find their 'yes' in Jesus (2 Cor 1:18). Hence the existence of Israel today is a sign in the midst of history of the continual dialectic between God's 'yes' and human beings' 'no'. God continues to say 'yes' but humankind has the possibility of saying 'no'. The conversion of Israel of which St Paul speaks in Romans 9 - 11 Balthasar reserves for the *eschaton*.

The other aspect of God's preparation for the fullness of time is his gift of the Spirit. Just as the Spirit opens the Trinity to the creation, so the Spirit is given in partial ways to humankind throughout its history. Through the Spirit God is offering himself to the world and seeking a human response of love. One of the signs of God's presence in Israel is the bestowal of the Spirit upon the prophets. But the more God offers himself the more humankind turns inward upon itself. The Spirit is the Spirit of promise, the Spirit who opens God's people to the future. Sin is the refusal of the promise which leads humankind to cling to its own present and to seek its own fulfilment. Finally in Jesus we see the man who both is filled with the

Spirit and in the power of the Spirit utters a perfect 'yes' to the Father. In this sense Jesus is the fullness of time. For in him God's purposes for the world are fulfilled. Jesus is at once the perfect offer of the Father and the perfect response to that offer. In him the *connubium* between God and the world is realized.

If it is the Spirit who opens up the future and if Jesus is permeated with the Spirit, then Jesus can also be said to be the future of the world. In Christ God has achieved his plan conceived before the foundation of the world. This is what we mean when we say that Jesus is the *eschaton*. In him eternity and time meet. The future of the world is already present. In a certain sense, a future beyond Jesus cannot be given. There is nothing more to await. As Balthasar puts it, 'Now, when absolute fullness has already been given, all that interpretation can do is to flow round it in never-ending circles, moving freely and without any compulsive line of development'.[10]

If this is the case, then we must ask: what sense does present time have for the Christian? Is the Spirit, given by Jesus to his Church, merely a Spirit who leads the Church into endless repetition of the past? Is not such a view of time too static, does it not rob humanity of the deepest dimension of temporality, namely the open space of the future into which ever new possibilities of creativity summon us?

THE ENIGMA OF TIME

In order to attempt a response to these questions, let us return anew to the fundamental problem of time and history from which we began. Let us then take our clue from Balthasar, and follow his circular method. In the manner of a fugue let us repeat the theme, but this time with a new variation. And as Balthasar would do, we can begin our reflection from below, examine the various dimensions of human temporality, all of which would seem to lead us into a cul-de-sac from which there is no exit. Then we can turn to Christ to see how he illumines the meaning of time and provides the key by which we can redeem it.

The problem of time is intimately linked to the status of human beings as creatures. As creatures they stand poised between the finite and the infinite. On the one hand they are drawn beyond themselves toward the Infinite. This infinity of transcendence makes all their human achievements appear infinitesimally small. Hence they are tempted to leave the world behind and seek a God beyond the world. At the same time, in spite of experiences of emptiness, boredom and loss of meaning, the world inevitably appears in our experience as valuable. In this world we daily encounter persons and things which we must affirm as true, good and beautiful. Hence the very desire to transcend the world presents us with the prospect of an enormous loss. Thus, every experience of love or beauty fills us with joy while at the same time it fills us with melancholy. For, on the one hand, as a finite love or beauty, it cannot fill the infinite space of our desires, and on the other hand the experience is as fleeting as it is beautiful and good. So the question which haunts humanity is this: how can people create something definitively valuable, of lasting worth, in a world where everything is in the process of perishing? If they leap toward God, they suffer the loss of the world. If they cling to finite realities, they block their transcendence.

The enigma is made ever more obscure if we take into account that not only is time a sign of finitude but that time as we live it is profoundly marked by sin. In the perspective of temporality, openness to God means precisely openness to his future, openness to the promise he makes and the fulfilment he offers. But each of us lives time in a different manner. We close in upon ourselves, put our faith in our own resources, seek our own fulfilment. We try to make our own future. But this very attempt tragically blocks the arrival of a genuine future. By grasping at our own future, we find ourselves locked in the past, condemned to repeat our past history. Sinful time is the vicious circle of the repetition of the past, a past that seems to offer a future but a future which turns out to be only a variation of the past. Hence not only is time a sign of finitude but sinful time bears all the marks of the frustration and destructiveness of turning away from God. Concretely in history after the fall, human beings experience time as futility and vanity. We continually have the experience of being condemned to repeat the mistakes of the past. We seem to have no genuine future. And so the question of time becomes ever more acute: can God redeem the time, can he give the irrevocability of the past a new possibility?

The fundamental answer which Balthasar offers to our question is Augustinian. Augustine's approach is to insert our human time into God's time. No solution to the problem of time can be found in the horizontal movement of chronological time toward the future. Rather, as Balthasar says, 'The extended structure of time can only be dissolved *vertically*, by being reinfolded in the freedom of transcending love'.[11] Hence the Augustinian solution is basically christological. Christ descends into time and redeems our time from within. Since Jesus is the divine Logos made flesh, every moment of his existence is filled with eternity. Time is no longer futile. Once again Balthasar finds the key in Jesus' obedience. Every moment of Jesus' human life is lived from the Father. Every instant offers him the possibility of a free response to the Father's love. Especially important here is the Johannine notion of Jesus' hour. Jesus lives always toward his hour, but he does not grasp it or try to anticipate it. He receives it as a gift from the Father. But having said all this, we must add another crucial dimension. Christ embraces not only finite time but sinful time as well. He embraces the human condition of the sinner so radically that he descends even into the realm of the dead. As we saw in developing the theology of Holy Saturday, Jesus becomes a cadaver-obedience for our sake. But in embracing even the 'no-time' of hell, Jesus redeems sinful time from within. Even the irrevocable past of sin is given a new future. Hell, which is precisely the absence of all possibilities and the land of complete hopelessness, is given the possibility of resurrection. The man condemned by sin to repeat his past is gifted to become the new creation.

THE TIME OF THE CHURCH

The fundamental meaning of time for the Christian community is the presence of the risen Christ in its midst. Balthasar in his theology of history places the emphasis on realized eschatology. The Christian need not look for some future event still outstanding in horizontal time, for the Bridegroom is already present with the bride here under the conditions of space and time. The chief sign of this presence is found in the sacraments, especially in the eucharist. Every time the Christian community celebrates eucharist it realizes the union between God and humanity and thus fulfils God's plan in creating the world. Christ is really present with his Church, although his presence is hidden under sacramental signs. Balthasar's theological aesthetics has shown that every revelation of God's presence is at the same time a veiling. In the incarnation God reveals himself but he becomes so human that he hides himself in the flesh. The same is true for his presence in the Church and in the eucharist. Although he is hidden, he is really present and the eyes of faith can see him. Thus he who encounters the risen Christ with faith experiences time not as empty and futile but as full of presence.

It would be one-sided, however, to speak of Christ's presence in the Church without speaking as well of the Holy Spirit. For the Christ who dwells in the community is precisely the pneumatic

Christ. Christ descended into the flesh to ascend with humanity to the Father. Thus the paschal mystery completes itself with the pouring out of the Holy Spirit who makes possible both Christ's indwelling in the community and the ascent of the community and indeed of all humanity to the Father. In speaking of the role of the Holy Spirit in the Church, Balthasar stresses both an objective and a subjective dimension. The objective dimension has its origin in the fact that the Holy Spirit is always the Spirit of Christ. As Jesus says, 'He will take what is mine and declare it to you' (John 16:14). Hence it is the task of the Holy Spirit to guarantee Christ's presence to the community. This he does in four ways: through the ordained ministry, the teaching office, the sacraments and Scripture. But these institutional aspects of the Holy Spirit do not exhaust his reality. The Holy Spirit is precisely the Spirit of freedom. Already in the Trinity we saw that the love of the Father and the Son is so great as to be ecstatic. Hence the Spirit of God is *Spiritus Creator*. Likewise we can say that the Christ-event as the revelation of the Father is a mystery of inexhaustible depth. In the time after Christ, while history continues, the Spirit, with a never-ending and unpredictable creativity, interprets this event to the world. Especially important here is the role of the saints. God raises up men and women in every age with special graces and missions for the Church and for humanity. Saints such as Francis of Assisi and Ignatius of Loyola as well as men and women of our own time such as Pope John XXIII or Mother Teresa are given to the Church by the Holy Spirit because God wishes to do something new in the world. The institutional Church has the obligation to heed these gifts of the Spirit. On the one hand, such sendings do not transcend the Christ-event, for in some way they recall Jesus and make him present. But on the other hand, there is in each of these missions a genuine novelty. Nevertheless, there is no contradiction here, for the mystery of Christ is inexhaustible.

If then we define human being-in-the-world as openness to the future, and if there is freedom only where there is genuine possibility, we can conclude that Christian existence in the Spirit is precisely openness to the future. For a Christian this future is both known and unknown. On the one hand, the world has no other future than Christ, and this future is opened up to us by the Spirit of Christ whom we have received in baptism. But on the other hand, the future of the world remains unknown in that where the Spirit will lead us in his unpredictable freedom remains hidden from our eyes. The Christian does not have a blueprint for the future of the world.

Rather what is important for believers is the liberty of Sonship by which they are open to the promptings of the Spirit, wherever they may lead.

THE MEANING OF TIME FOR THE CHRISTIAN

What then is the meaning of time for the Christian? If the end has been realized, why does history continue? Why does Christ not come again? Obviously it is impossible for human reason to given an adequate answer to such questions. The answer is hidden in the mystery of God's providence. Balthasar prefers to appeal to images.

One important image for him is that of the seed hidden in the ground. Already in the synoptic gospels we find the parable of the Kingdom as seed scattered upon the ground (see Mark 4:26–29). The man who plants the seed sleeps while the earth of itself brings forth fruit, first the blade, then the ear, then the full grain in the ear. Dear to Balthasar's heart is the Johannine version of the metaphor according to which the seed must fall into the ground and die in order to produce much fruit (John 12:24). With the coming of Christ and his death and resurrection, the Kingdom of God has been planted. The victory has been won. It is not up to us to seize the victory. Rather we are called to plant the seeds of the Kingdom and to let God produce the harvest as he will. According to this image, the sense of time is that of sowing the seed, most often in hiddenness. As Balthasar puts it, 'All our temporal life is Advent: bearing fruit in patience without the curiosity to want to see with our eyes the success of our life of faith'.[12]

Another key image to which Balthasar appeals is that of the bride and the bridegroom. The time which Christ has given us is the time of his wooing of the bride. In this sense the real drama of history is not the conflict between God and Satan but the struggle between Christ and his Church. The bride is not yet purified, is not yet the spouse without spot and wrinkle (Eph 5:27). The love of the bride is still too tepid. Hence the bridegroom tarries. The meaning of time is thus the call to love, for only a more intensive love on the part of the bride can hasten the coming of the bridegroom.

What then is the bride summoned to do? Once again, as so often with Balthasar, the images to which he appeals are feminine. The bride is certainly not called to force the hand of the bridegroom, nor even primarily to *do* something. Rather the bride is called to *be*: to wait, to keep vigil, and to remain ever more firmly rooted in him.

'Abide in my love' (John 15:9): this is the meaning of temporal existence. Only in this abiding is the extendedness of horizontal time unified by being enfolded in the vertical dimension of trinitarian love. Such abiding may seem excessively passive. But here too Christ challenges our masculine attitudes of productivity and achievement. Christ accomplished the redemption of the world in the utter helplessness of the cross. Faith challenges us to believe that the more deeply we are inserted into him, the more radically we abide in him, so much richer will be the fruit which the vine produces. In this sense there is no greater activity or apostolate than the contemplative receptivity of 'abiding'.

THE END OF THE DRAMA

According to Balthasar, the Christian understanding of time is dialectical. There is a horizontal movement forward and a vertical movement upwards. As far as the horizontal movement is concerned, Balthasar would argue that we cannot really speak of progress in history. As he puts it, 'In a hundred thousand years, humanity will not be one inch closer to the archetype Christ than it is today'.[13] The reason for this is the mystery of freedom. In a certain sense the drama of history begins over again with the birth of every person.

Thus he would maintain that we cannot expect any inner-worldly fulfilment of history. In a confrontation with Marxist utopian thinkers such as Ernst Bloch (1885–1977), Balthasar argues that the idea of an inner-worldly fulfilment of history is contradictory. Such a vision of utopia must inevitably be collectivist. This type of philosophy necessarily sees the fulfilment in terms of the progress of medicine, cybernetics, sociology and so on. But none of these categorical objectivizations of human beings can do justice to the mystery of their freedom. Bloch defines utopia as 'the identity of man with himself'. But Balthasar asks if such a definition does not contradict the true nature of the human, namely openness to the genuinely new. As long as humans are human, no identity with themselves is possible. Indeed, in Balthasar's opinion, the realization of such an identity would be equivalent to the classical definition of hell, namely persons closed in upon themselves.

Nonetheless, Balthasar believes that our human history will have an end. What this end will be is unpredictable but Balthasar is pessimistic as regards prospects for the future. Here his imagination is shaped by the apocalyptic literature of the Bible. He argues that a belief in evolution is by no means incompatible with an apocalyptic end to history. For evolution brings with it the development of technology and its ever greater means of destruction. Who is to control these weapons of death? As long as the human heart remains unconverted, the evolution of intelligence is accompanied by a corresponding threat of disaster. And Christian faith is no guarantee of a happy end to the story.

Where then is Christian hope centred? Is the hope of final victory certain? Or can hope, as Bloch would argue, be disappointed? Balthasar would answer that our hope is indeed certain, but that the true hope of Christians lies in the vertical ascent toward the Father. Beyond the possibility of inner-worldly catastrophe lies the hope of the incommensurable future which consists in the resurrection of the dead and the journey of Christ toward the Father. Believers have already set out on this journey. They are already in union with Christ. With death the thin veil which separates the believer from the sight of the Lord will be taken away. On the one hand, death thus means the unveiling of the bridegroom. On the other hand it means the arrival at the goal, an arrival which constitutes a new beginning. Balthasar describes this goal as *connubium*, the bridal union between the creature and God. This union represents the fullness of communion between I and Thou. It is no mystical dissolution of the I in the One. Nor can such a communion be conceived as static. If it were, the utopian philosophers would be correct and Christian faith would contradict the essence of the human. Rather faith reaches its goal when in consummation it begins its unending journey into the infinite Mystery of God. In the Spirit the person journeys through Christ to the ever greater source of love who is the Father.

Notes

1 *Theologik* I (Einsiedeln: Johannes, 1985), p. 118.

2 See *Theologik* II (Einsiedeln: Johannes, 1985), pp. 51ff.

3 See ibid., p. 150.

4 *The God of Jesus Christ* (London: SCM Press, 1984), p. 226.

5 'Eschatologie im Umriss' in *Pneuma und Institution* (Einsiedeln: Johannes, 1974), p. 451.

6 See Balthasar, *Man in History* (London: Sheed and Ward, 1982), pp. 165ff., 181ff.

7 See Chapter 3, note 14.

8 The Encompassing is one of the expressions which Jaspers employs to indicate Being itself, or God within whom human transcendence moves and toward whom it is oriented.

9 See *The Glory of the Lord* 1, pp. 495ff.

10 *Theology of History* (London: Sheed and Ward, 1963), p. 136.

11 *Man in History*, p. 19.

12 *Du krönst das Jahr mit deiner Huld* (Einsiedeln: Johannes, 1982), p. 228.

13 Ibid., p. 219.

13

Contemplation in action

Once in an interview the Jesuit theologian Karl Rahner was asked who was the person who had most influenced his theology. The interviewer expected some such name as Kant, Maréchal or Heidegger. Instead Rahner replied: St Ignatius of Loyola. The same, I think, could be said of Hans Urs von Balthasar. He is *par excellence* an Ignatian theologian, and no theme stands more at the centre of his theology than that of being a contemplative in action, the ideal which Ignatius proposes for the exercitant at the end of the *Spiritual Exercises* when he develops the contemplation to obtain the love of God.

It has often been noted that the differences between Rahner and Balthasar are profound, especially as regards method. Balthasar could never tolerate Rahner's transcendental method which seemed to him a Procrustean bed in which Christianity had to be reduced in size in order to find a place. Moreover, Balthasar's entire theology is much more oriented to the paschal mystery than is Rahner's and he often argued that Rahner's whole frame of reference lacked the dramatic dimension and thus eclipsed the cross which is the culmination of the interaction of divine and human freedom.[1]

Nonetheless, as regards the central vision of finding God in all things, Balthasar and Rahner are profoundly in harmony. One of Rahner's most beautiful essays, brief in its extension and more than ordinarily clear in its content is 'The Ignatian mysticism of joy in the world'.[2] In this essay Rahner asks how we can make sense out of the seemingly contradictory experience of the early Jesuits who, on the one hand, built splendid Baroque churches, wrote dramas, studied

154

the rapidly developing sciences such as astronomy, and at the same time sent men to the missions prepared to die agonizingly for Christ in the boiling fountains of Japan or the bamboo cages of Tonkin. If there is an Ignatian mysticism of the world, surely these paradoxes of early Jesuit experience cannot be explained by a facile optimism about the course of the cosmos and the future of history.

Rahner suggests, that however strange it may seem, Ignatius's love for the world has its deepest foundations in the flight from the world which characterized the early monastic experiences in Christianity. The monks fled from the world or were crucified to the world because the God they worshipped was beyond the world. The same is true for Ignatius. God is so transcendent that he must be loved beyond all things. This transcendence grounds the notion of indifference in regard to creatures, which is the hallmark of the 'Principle and Foundation' of the *Spiritual Exercises*. But, on the other hand, the very transcendence of God, his infinite freedom, makes possible his entrance into the world in the act of the Incarnation. And God is so free that he not only can exist among us bodily but he can also take upon himself our deepest darkness, the obscure night of abandonment on the cross. This paradox of divine transcendence and immanence grounds the Ignatian mysticism of joy in the world. Since God is the ever-greater one, the Christian is summoned to a freedom which is ready to do the divine will and thus to find God wherever the Lord wishes to send him. And this can be in the palaces of the princes, in the lecture halls of the University, but equally among the Iroquois of North America or the peasants of the Paraguay reductions.

These insights developed by Rahner are totally in harmony with the central thrust of Balthasar's theology. No phrase is more central to Balthasar's thought than *Deus semper maior* (the ever greater God). God always exceeds any of our expectations. Hence if it is true, as Gerard Manley Hopkins says, that the world is charged with the grandeur of God, it is even more true to say that God's glory is infinitely greater than the tiny reflection we find of it in creation.

Since God is *Deus semper maior* the only fitting attitude before him is that of obedience. For Balthasar, as we have seen in our study of his Christology, the primordial example of this obedience is Jesus Christ. And Christ's obedience does not have its point of departure in his earthly mission but already characterized his life in the eternal Trinity. It is this obedience which opens Jesus to mission. And it is this obedience which makes Jesus the perfect contemplative in action. He can find God at any moment, for he seeks nothing other than the will of the Father. So open is Jesus to mission that he can even find God in the darkest moment of the Father's apparent absence on the cross.

These christological insights form the foundations of Balthasar's approach to spirituality, and here it is important to remember that Balthasar never saw his life's work as theology for the sake of theology. The chief desire of his heart was to work for the renewal of the Church. This explains his lifelong commmitment to giving the *Spiritual Exercises*, his work as a translator of the Christian classics, his desire to overcome the dichotomy between theology and spirituality and, finally, his enormous sense of mission as regards founding the secular institute of the Community of St John which would have as its goal the living of Ignatian spirituality in the world. Balthasar regarded this institute as a deepening of the Ignatian insights for our time; in other words, he wanted a group of men and women not just living the evangelical counsels in the world, but living them in a hidden way trusting in God alone to give their lives fecundity. At the heart of this entire project is Balthasar's deepest conviction that only Christianity does full justice to the reality of the world, for Christian faith alone offers a way of salvation which does not consist in denying the world but in redeeming and sanctifying it. If Christ himself did not shrink from becoming body in space and time, then we too must redeem the time. Each of us is called to do this in a way chosen by God alone and revealed to us in prayer. Here once again the key themes of the Ignatian *Exercises*: election and mission.

What then does it mean for Balthasar to be a contemplative in action? How are we to understand the relationship between contemplation and action? Balthasar already expressed himself beautifully on this point in an essay 'Action and contemplation', written while still a Jesuit in 1948 and later reprinted in *Verbum Caro*.[3] Let us follow him as he tries to unravel the threads of the problem which has haunted all the religions and indeed the Christian faith from the beginning of its history.

First of all, he notes that the two concepts 'contemplation' and 'action' are not as such contradictories, as would be for example the ideas of action and passion.

Secondly, he wishes to confront the problem: in what sense can we or should we say that the contemplative life is higher than the active life? Here he argues that we must proceed with extreme caution. If by 'contemplative life' we mean the life of the human spirit, then we must indeed say that this life is its own goal. *Homo sapiens* (man as spirit) cannot be reduced to *homo faber* (man as maker). A functionalization or instrumentalization of the human spirit means the dehumanization of the human person.

But, thirdly, Balthasar alerts us to the acute danger of an excessive Hellenization of the problem which has infected the Christian tradition and has at times brought with it anti-Christian attitudes and practices. By Hellenization Balthasar means the over-valuation of the eternal in contrast to the temporal. Only the eternal as such has a lasting value and the temporal can only have value by accident. Thus Aristotle judges contemplation to be the highest act of the human being, for this act most closely approaches the eternal. This attitude certainly affects many of the Fathers of the Church for whom contemplation is a sheer joy whereas activity is a burden to be borne by necessity. For these Fathers the Christian soul must long to be freed from the weight of history in order to enjoy the sheer bliss of eternity. One sees that the Greek interpretation of Christianity is a way of ascent whose goal is to leave the world behind as soon as possible.

In the Middle Ages, especially in the tradition of St Dominic, which was later developed theologically by St Thomas, there was a certain breakthrough in the Dominican ideal of handing on to others the fruits of contemplation (*contemplata aliis tradere*). Here more than in the Greek Fathers action as such became a value insofar as it flowed from contemplation (*ex plenitudine contemplationis derivatur*), and in this sense St Thomas argued that the mixed life of contemplation and action is higher than the contemplative life alone, for the mixed life in which contemplation issues in apostolic action brings souls to God. Nonetheless, in the end, St Thomas argued that the life of the hermit is the highest form of perfection, for the perfect man is sufficient unto himself, even if it is true that life in society was necessary first in order to bring him to this perfection. Here Balthasar observes that we see a much too individualistic conception of the person and of the meaning of salvation.

Two other accents in St Thomas still reflect an excessive Hellenization of the gospel. First, Thomas creates a hierarchy whereby contemplation is superior to action, for contemplation remains whereas action passes away. Thomas even makes an analogy between the hierarchy of contemplation over action and that of the man over the woman. But, as Balthasar comments, is the super-ordination of the man over the woman really a superiority? For does not the man need the woman in order to bear fruit? Does not the man remain sterile unless he dies to himself, passing through the door of woman? Is this not what St Paul means when he says that the woman is the glory of man?

Aquinas is also unduly influenced by the Greek mentality when he sharply divides the love of God from the love of neighbour, ranking the former superior to the latter. Balthasar asks if the love of which Paul speaks in 1 Corinthians 13 is not really the undivided love of God *and* neighbour.

In Balthasar's opinion all these difficulties can only be resolved by going back to the heart of the Christian revelation. There we see, in the first instance, that the life of the Trinity is as such a union of contemplation and action. The three persons exist in an unbroken gaze of love and yet they are supremely active in their mutual self-giving. Moreover, the contemplative gaze of love of the persons of the Trinity remains unbroken in their missions toward the world. Secondly, we have already noted how Christ's whole life is both contemplative and active. As St John puts it, he always does what he sees the Father doing. The interpenetration of activity and contemplation reaches its high point on the cross. There Jesus can do nothing more. He can only let it happen to him. But this passivity, even to the point of becoming a cadaver-obedience, contains in itself the superabundant fruitfulness which redeems the whole world. The fact that Jesus holds nothing back but opens himself without reserve makes possible a fecundity without limits.

Thus the ultimate resolution of the problem of contemplation and action must be that proposed by St Ignatius, that is, the interfusion and interpenetration of prayer and work, so that the Christian contemplative finds God in all things, as indeed Ignatius said that he could find God at any moment. This, then, is the goal of an Ignatian theology: to be with God in the world. In this approach there is no contradiction between prayer and apostolate but only the most fruitful tension.

To complete this picture of Balthasar's understanding of Christian spirituality, perhaps we could give the last word to fecundity. In Balthasar's opinion, if there is any saint who has advanced beyond Ignatius of Loyola, it is Thérèse of Lisieux who, though an enclosed nun, was correctly chosen to be patroness of the missions because of her apostolic prayer. So deep was her penetration into the mystery of God's love that she saw that all contemplation is in itself already fruitful. It is impossible to enter into the mystery of God's love in Christ without this love overflowing the vessel which receives it. Thus every prayer will be fruitful somewhere in the world. And the one who begins to enter more deeply into this mystery is carried imperceptibly to a profound disregard of self. Those who begin to love perforce cease to worry about their own happiness, are no longer concerned with merit, and even forget about heaven for themselves. Their whole being is caught up in the fact that everything is gift. And so they only wish to give as they have been given. As Thérèse put it in her autobiography, 'Not to accumulate provisions . . . To distribute one's goods as soon as one receives them. Even if one were to reach eighty years of age, still to be poor. Everything which one has, to immediately give it away.'[4] Such is the true understanding of Christian contemplation, an understanding which opens up a new perspective in which the apparent dichotomy between contemplation and action is resolved and the seeming conflict between prayer and apostolate ceases to be a problem.

Notes

1 See, for example, *Cordula oder der Ernstfall* (Einsiedeln: Johannes, 1966); also *Theodramatik* III (Einsiedeln: Johannes, 1980), pp. 253–62.

2 Karl Rahner, 'The Ignatian mysticism of joy in the world' in *Theological Investigations* 3 (London: Darton, Longman and Todd, 1967), pp. 277–93.

3 'Aktion und Kontemplation' in *Verbum Caro* (Einsiedeln: Johannes, 1960), pp. 245–59.

4 Cited by Balthasar, ibid., p. 259.

Index

Abraham 40
Absolute
 in Western philosophy 6
 Hegelian 13–14
 and see God
Adam 25
 first and second 111
 and see fall
admirabile commercium 101, 124
aesthetics
 faith an aesthetic act 8, 19–21, 31, 32,
  32n, 40
 theological 18–34, 37, 91, 148
 in Catholic theology 20
 rejected by Protestants 19–20
agape 32
alienation, human 56
analogy
 'hovering' 55
 and see Beauty; Being; faith; form
anima/animus 30, 34n
Anselm viii, 90, 102, 105
anthropology 25, 49, 50
 and eucharist 121
 Luther's 104
 Rahner's 105
 and sacrifice 123
anti-Christ, Barthian 4
apostasy 88
Aquinas, Thomas 33n, 64, 67, 68, 90,
  125n, 142–3, 157–8
Aristotle 33n, 144, 157
Arnold, Matthew 112
art 22, 30, 60, 72
 analogy of 28, 30
 and see aesthetics; form
atheism 7, 15–16, 68
Augustine 40, 89, 101, 116, 119, 120, 122,
  147
autoexousios (of the human being) 68
autonomy (of creature) 67–9, 71, 131

Balthasar, Hans Urs von
 biographical details 1–3
 central insights and interest 6–8, 9n,
  18–19
 'elitist' 7
 Christology 35–53, 156

soteriology 108–13
 universalist 3
 and see individual topics of theological
  interest
baptism 24, 41, 84, 87, 111, 149, 120,
  125n, 134, 149
Barth, Karl
 influence on Balthasar 4–5, 20–1; on
  Girard 107, 114n
 theology 4–5, 16, 20, 77, 91, 108
Basel, University of 1
Beauty
 analogy of 30
 divine 18, 20–1, 32n, 139
 experienced in the world 147
 rejected by Protestant theology 20
Being
 analogy of 4–5, 11, 30, 33n, 42, 111
 in Balthasar's theology 6, 10, 30
 ground of 68–9
 revelation of 14, 17, 26, 30, 52
 self-disclosing 139–40
 transcendental 7–8, 139
 as trinitarian love 6–7, 9n, 28
 and see God; Spirit
Benedictines, Order of 1
Berlin 1
Bernanos, Georges 2
Bible 20, 152
 and see Old Testament; Scripture
Bloch, Ernst 151
Bloy, Léon 121
bodiliness 5, 57, 110, 116
Bonaventure 142
bride, image of 23, 34n, 99, 117–20, 136
Buddhism 16, 57, 63, 69
Bultmann, Rudolf 27, 33n, 34n, 37

cadaver-obedience 158
Calvin, John 5
caritas 7, 135
Casel, Odo 126n
catechists, lay 134
catharsis 106, 110, 114n
catholicity 8, 10–17, 144
Catholics 1, 2
celibacy 133
Chalcedon, Council of 46

160

INDEX

analogy of 4–5, 21, 33n, 42
as call to decision 37
contemplative function 19, 23–4, 75, 91
and culture 2
darkness of 40–1
feminine dimension 123–5
Jesus' 39–40, 47
and knowledge of God 4
Mary's 5
in the Old Testament 40
surrender 75
trinitarian 75
and see Christoformic
fall 111, 128–9, 147
in Gnostics and Plato 54
in poets and philosophers 63
Fathers, Church
influence on Balthasar 3, 5
on contemplation 157
on faith 24, 124
on Incarnation 79
on *imago Dei* 111
on Mary 22, 117
on original human state 128
on Trinity 77n, 79
universalism 52
and see individual Fathers; patristics
fecundity
in marriage 143
spiritual 9n, 23, 128, 131, 156, 158
feminine dimension 120, 123–4
and see Mary
Feuerbach, Ludwig Andreas 10–11
fideism 22
finitude, human 54–5, 60, 140, 145
form (*Gestalt*)
of the beautiful 21
of the Church 115, 125n
of the Father 28, 31
of Jesus Christ 22–3, 28, 27, 29, 30
Jesus' form impressed on believer 22–3
in the New Testament 37
formlessness, of Christ 31–2
forty days, theology of 96–7
Fourth Lateran Council 4
Francis of Assisi 133, 149
freedom
within the Church 135
divine and human 5, 8, 54, 65–78, 89,
107, 110, 113, 121, 128, 129, 155
and eucharist 121
in Hegel 141–2
meaning and mystery 54, 67, 140
of Sonship 150
trinitarian 74–7
involved with truth 139
Freud, Sigmund 57, 106, 114n

Ganze, das (Christ) 11
Gehenna 86
Gethsemane 40, 81–2, 131–2
Girard, René 105–8, 110, 114n
glory, divine 8, 42, 46
contemplation of 19, 21
revealed in Jesus 42
reflected in created world 4, 155
gnosticism, modern 27
Gnostics 54, 63
God
Absolute Spirit 6
supreme Beauty 18

in Christ the Son 18–19, 28, 100
revealed as Creator 56, 92
Deus semper maior 15
faithful 40, 71, 79, 85
freedom 65, 69–72
immutable 70
justice and mercy 82–3, 114n
immanent 155
liberator, redeemer and saviour 3, 54,
102–3, 131
monadic, monotheistic 16–17
in Old Testament 39, 45, 56
Other/Not Other 66
and prayer 97
revelation to creature 4, 5, 11, 15, 27,
32, 33n, 71, 73, 97, 99, 145
self-expression, self-giving, self-presence,
self-revelation 6, 13, 23, 25, 142
beyond sexuality 57
in space and time 21
and the Spirit 39, 145
suffering 54
super-form 76
transcendence 11, 57, 71, 155,
veiled 148
wrath 85–6
and see glory; grace; Holy Trinity;
incarnation; Israel
gods, pagan 10–11, 26, 28, 33n, 39, 55, 57
good, the 8, 68
Good Friday 84–5, 88
gospels 4, 37–8, 39, 41, 150
grace 3, 23, 112
Luther on 125, 126n
in *nouvelle théologie* 3
sacramental 132
Gregory Nazianzen 101
Gregory of Nyssa
influence on Balthasar 3
on human person 68
on the Incarnation 46, 79
and 'totality' 52
Greshake, Gisbert 121
Gügler, Alois 20

Hartshorne, Charles 77n
hearing–seeing dichotomy 19
Hebrews *see* Israel; Judaism
Hebrews, letter to the 88, 124
Hegel, G. W. F. 11, 13–14, 17
criticized by Balthasar 13–14
on Being 140–2
on freedom 65–6
on God and suffering 108
on love 140
on sexuality and death 58
Heidegger, Martin 6, 30, 62, 139–42
hell 85–7
Christ's descent to 35, 148
classical definition of 151
second 88–90
and see Sheol
Hellenization, danger of 157
Heschel, Abraham 15
historical, history 23, 143–4
Jesus Christ in 16, 27, 29, 37, 144–5
historisch and *geschichtlich* 91–2
and realized eschatology 147
salvation history 8
telos of 144
and time 146–50

162